WILLIAMS-SONOMA
GRANDE CUISINE
P9-DHQ-387

Ice Creams & Sorbets

General Editor
Chuck Williams

Recipes
Sarah Tenaglia

Photography
Allan Rosenberg

TIME-LIFE BOOKS
Time-Life Books is a division of Time Life Inc.
Time-Life is a trademark of Time Warner Inc. U.S.A.

Time-Life Custom Publishing
Vice President and Publisher: Terry Newell
Vice President of Sales and Marketing: Neil Levin
Director of Financial Operations: J. Brian Birky
Director of Acquisitions: Jennifer L. Pearce

WILLIAMS-SONOMA
Founder and Vice Chairman: Chuck Williams
Associate Book Buyer: Cecilia Michaelis

WELDON OWEN INC.
President: John Owen
Vice President and Publisher: Wendely Harvey
Chief Operating Officer: Larry Partington
Vice President International Sales: Stuart Laurence
Associate Publisher: Laurie Wertz
Managing Editor: Lisa Chaney Atwood
Consulting Editor: Norman Kolpas
Copy Editor: Sharon Silva
Design: John Bull, The Book Design Company
Production Director: Stephanie Sherman
Production Coordinator: Tarji Mickelson
Production Editor: Janique Gascoigne
Food Photographer: Allan Rosenberg
Additional Food Photography: Allen V. Lott
Primary Food Stylist: Heidi Gintner
Primary Prop Stylist: Sandra Griswold
Assistant Food Stylists: Nette Scott, Elizabeth C. Davis
Assistant Prop Stylist: Elizabeth C. Davis
Glossary Illustrations: Alice Harth

The Williams-Sonoma Kitchen Library
conceived and produced by Weldon Owen Inc.
814 Montgomery St., San Francisco, CA 94133

In collaboration with Williams-Sonoma
3250 Van Ness Ave., San Francisco, CA 94109

Printed in China by Toppan Printing Co., LTD.

A Note on Weights and Measures:
All recipes include customary U.S. and metric measurements. Metric conversions are based on a standard developed for these books and have been rounded off. Actual weights may vary.

A Weldon Owen Production

Reprinted in 1996; 1996; 1998; 1999

Library of Congress
Cataloging-in-Publication Data:

Tenaglia, Sarah.
Ice Creams & sorbets / general editor, Chuck Williams : recipes, Sarah Tenaglia ; photography, Allan Rosenberg.
p. cm. — (Williams-Sonoma kitchen library)
ISBN 0-7835-0310-5
1. Ice cream, ices, etc. I. Williams, Chuck. II. Title. III. Series.
TX795.T27 1996
641.8'62—dc20 95-32823
CIP

Contents

Introduction

A hot summer's day fading to evening. A churn on the back porch, laboriously cranked in its bed of crushed ice and rock salt. The incomparable delight of scooping thick, creamy frozen vanilla custard off the paddle just an instant after it has been pulled from the tub.

Even if we've never made it the old-fashioned way, such snapshots of memory are embedded in our consciousness, so elemental are the pleasures of good ice cream. And today, kitchen countertop ice cream machines make it possible to achieve those pleasures without aching arms or mounds of ice and salt.

The ease with which anyone can make good, homemade frozen desserts is the reason behind this book, which brings together 44 kitchen-tested recipes for ice creams, frozen mousses, sorbets and sherbets, granitas and gelati. To give you further help in achieving perfect results, there is a step-by-step guide to making each of these basic types of frozen dessert, as well as suggestions and recipes for serving and embellishing them with flair.

Look through these recipes now and I am sure you'll be impressed by how easy they are, and how few ingredients you need to make them. (Happily absent are all those scientific-sounding compounds—stabilizers, artificial flavorings and the like—you see listed on the packages of some commercial products.)

This book aims to put the old-fashioned joys of making frozen desserts within the reach of any home cook. And, for all the improvements in the process, one important thing hasn't changed: You still have the pleasure of eating fresh-churned ice cream right off the paddle the moment the job is done!

Equipment

Basic tools for mixing, freezing, shaping and serving all kinds of ice creams, sorbets, sherbets, granitas and gelati

The equipment shown here will enable you to produce results in your home kitchen every bit as polished as those of the grandest ice cream parlor. From saucepans for cooking custards to sieves for ensuring a smooth consistency, machines for freezing to containers and scoops for storing and serving, every piece should be readily available in any well-stocked cookware shop.

Although ice cream machines vary widely according to size, price and the amount of time it takes to produce perfectly frozen results, any electric or hand-churned machine will work for the recipes in this book.

1. Kitchen Towel
For general kitchen cleanup. Also, formed into a ring and placed on a work surface, steadies metal bowl while ingredients are whisked together.

2. Food Processor
For puréeing fruit; puréeing partially frozen mixtures; or chopping nuts, chocolate or other ingredients.

3. Electric Mixer
Heavy-duty, variable-speed countertop mixer with stainless-steel bowl for beating ingredients for frozen mousses.

4. Saucepans
For heating milk or cream, heating and thickening ice cream custard mixtures, and cooking fruits with sugar for making sorbets or sherbets.

5. Sieves
Large medium-mesh sieve removes lumps from custard for making ice cream; small fine-mesh sieve is ideal for dusting cocoa powder.

6. Baking Sheet
Large baking sheet allows nuts to be spread in a single layer for toasting.

7. Cheesecloth
For enclosing whole spices when simmered in sorbet or other frozen dessert mixtures, facilitating easy removal. Muslin can also be used.

8. Rubber Spatula
For folding ingredients together and pressing liquids from solids when straining purées.

9. Wooden Spatula
For stirring custard mixtures as they heat and thicken.

10. Pastry Brush
For brushing down pan sides when making sugar syrups.

11. Measuring Cups and Spoons
Lip and handle on heavy-duty, heat-resistant glass measuring

cup ensures easy pouring of liquid ingredients. Straight rims of calibrated metal spoons and cups in graduated sizes allow dry ingredients to be leveled for accuracy.

12. Parchment Paper
For cutting into strips to be used as collars for supporting mousse mixtures in serving cups during freezing.

13. Paring Knife
For peeling and cutting up fruit, chopping small ingredients, splitting and scraping vanilla beans, or loosening the edges of some frozen desserts before unmolding.

14. Serrated Knife
For slicing unmolded frozen desserts and cutting up large ingredients.

15. Stripper
Thin, curved edge at end of stainless-steel blade cuts citrus zest into long, thin strips.

16. Peeler
For all-purpose peeling of fruit and for removing wide strips of citrus zest.

17. Candy Thermometer
For gauging the temperature of some ice cream toppings and dessert mixtures as they cook.

18. Shredder
Small, hand-held shredder has tiny cutting holes for finely shredding citrus zest.

19. Wire Whisk
For beating together sugar and egg yolks and whisking granita mixtures during the freezing process.

20. Rectangular Container
Tempered-glass loaf pan and plastic lid can be used as a freezer container for ice cream and other frozen desserts, or for molding ice cream assemblies.

21. Mixing Bowls
Sturdy plastic bowls in a range of sizes for all-purpose mixing. Lips enable easy pouring.

22. Electric Ice Cream Makers
Advanced electric refrigeration model mixes and freezes frozen dessert mixtures in its own built-in chamber. Less expensive, cylindrical model features a refrigerant-filled tub that is frozen in the home freezer before a frozen dessert mixture is added for processing.

23. Coarse Sieve
For straining custard mixtures, seeds from berry purées, and for general straining purposes.

24. Metal Mixing Bowl
For quick freezing of granita mixtures and whisking together eggs and sugar.

25. Ring Mold
For molding frozen desserts.

26. Metal Loaf Pan
For molding layered frozen dessert presentations.

27. Springform Pan
Circular pan with spring-clip sides that loosen for easy unmolding of ice cream cakes. Available in a range of sizes, but usually comes 9 inches (23 cm) in diameter and 2–3 inches (5–7.5 inches) deep.

28. Freezer Containers
Freezerproof plastic containers with airtight lids, for storing frozen desserts.

29. Ice Cream Scoops
For all-purpose scooping and serving of frozen desserts.

Ice Cream Basics

The eight photographs and captions on the opposite page take you step-by-step through the making of a classic vanilla bean ice cream. With minimal variations, all revolving around the additions of fruit, chocolate or other flavorings, the same procedures apply to any of the custard-based ice cream recipes on pages 17–50 as well as to the recipes on pages 65–72 for the denser, generally richer Italian ice cream known as gelato.

Whichever recipe you use, pay careful attention to including the precise measurements indicated for each ingredient. Any changes you make in the amount of sugar, or any addition of extra ingredients that contain alcohol, could adversely affect the frozen consistency of the ice cream. Bear in mind that the mixture will taste sweeter before freezing than after. Take care, as well, to follow the instructions for whatever type of ice cream maker you use; and, unless you prefer the consistency of soft-serve ice cream, allow sufficient time for the finished product to harden in your freezer.

Vanilla Bean Ice Cream

Classic Vanilla Bean Ice Cream

The best vanilla ice cream is made with vanilla beans that have been steeped in custard to release their maximum flavor. If vanilla beans are unavailable, simply omit the steeping and add 2 teaspoons vanilla extract (essence) to the chilled custard before freezing.

3 cups (24 fl oz/750 ml) half-and-half (half cream)
1 vanilla bean
¾ cup (6 oz/185 g) sugar
6 egg yolks

Pour the half-and-half into a medium-sized, heavy saucepan. Place the vanilla bean on a work surface. Using a small, sharp knife, cut the bean in half lengthwise. Using the knife tip, scrape the seeds from the vanilla bean, then add the seeds and bean halves to the half-and-half. Bring to a simmer over medium-high heat. Remove from the heat. Cover and let stand for 30 minutes.

Return the saucepan to the stove top over medium-high heat and again bring to a simmer. Meanwhile, in a metal bowl, whisk together the sugar and yolks until blended. Form a kitchen towel into a ring and place the bowl on top to prevent it from moving. Gradually pour the hot half-and-half mixture into the yolk mixture, whisking constantly. Return the mixture to the same saucepan and place over medium-low heat. Cook, stirring slowly and continuously with a wooden spatula, until the custard thickens and leaves a path on the back of the spatula when a finger is drawn across it, about 5 minutes; do not allow to boil.

Pour the custard through a medium-mesh sieve set over a clean bowl. Refrigerate until cold, about 1 hour.

Transfer the custard to an ice cream maker and process according to the manufacturer's instructions. Transfer the ice cream to a container; cover and freeze until firm, at least 4 hours or for up to 3 days.

Makes about 5 cups (1.25 l); serves 8

MAKING ICE CREAM

1. Scraping the vanilla bean. Use a small, sharp knife to cut the vanilla bean in half lengthwise. With the tip of the knife, scrape out and reserve the small, dark seeds clustered inside the bean halves.

2. Heating the half-and-half. Add the vanilla seeds and bean halves to the saucepan of half-and-half and bring to a simmer, heating it just until bubbles appear at the pan's edge. Remove from the heat, cover and let steep for 30 minutes, then return to a simmer.

3. Steadying the bowl. In a metal bowl, whisk together the sugar and egg yolks. Form a kitchen towel into a ring on a work surface. Place the bowl in the center of the ring to prevent it from moving while ingredients are mixed.

4. Combining the ingredients. Whisking continuously, gradually add the hot half-and-half mixture to the egg yolk mixture to form a custard.

5. Cooking the custard. Return the mixture to the same saucepan. Place over the heat and cook, stirring with a wooden spatula, until the custard thickens sufficiently to leave a path when you draw your finger across the back of the spatula, about 5 minutes.

6. Straining the custard. Set a medium-mesh sieve over a clean bowl. Pour the custard through the sieve to remove the vanilla pods and eliminate any lumps; then refrigerate the custard until cold, about 1 hour.

7. Freezing the ice cream. Transfer the cold custard to an ice cream maker and process according to manufacturer's instructions. Transfer the ice cream to a freezer container and place in the freezer until firm.

8. Serving the ice cream. Remove the ice cream from the freezer and let it soften slightly, if necessary. Serve with an ice cream scoop, dipping the utensil into a bowl of hot water if necessary to aid in scooping.

Sorbets, Sherbets & Granitas

These three types of frozen desserts are distinguished from ice creams, gelati and frozen mousses in that they often highlight the flavor of fruit and do not include either egg yolks or cream.

Sorbets are traditionally based on a sugar-and-water syrup, to which puréed fruit or other natural flavoring is added. Sherbets can also include a sugar syrup as well as milk or yogurt and, in the recipes in this book, gelatin. Both sorbets and sherbets should be processed in an ice cream maker for the best consistency.

Granitas, however, are frozen in plain metal bowls in the freezer. The simple sugar-and-water syrup on which they are based, and the process of scraping them with a fork before serving, yield the pleasantly grainy consistency from which their name derives.

Mango Sorbet

Sorbet

Sorbet is characterized by its dense, smooth texture and wonderfully intense flavor—often one of fresh fruit. Sorbet is usually based on pulverized fruit and sweeteners in the form of simple syrup and corn syrup or, here, as a mixture of sugar and corn syrup.

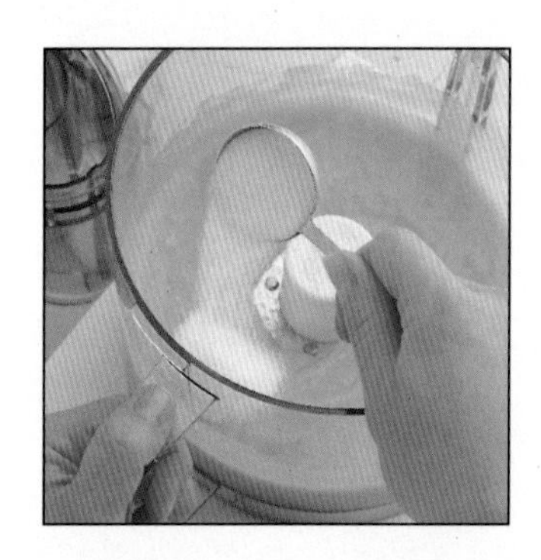

1. Combining the ingredients. Place the fruit—here, mango—in a food processor and process until smooth. Add the sugar and corn syrup and process until thoroughly blended. Transfer to a bowl, cover and refrigerate until cold.

2. Freezing the sorbet. Place the purée in an ice cream maker and process according to manufacturer's instructions. Transfer to a freezer container and freeze until firm.

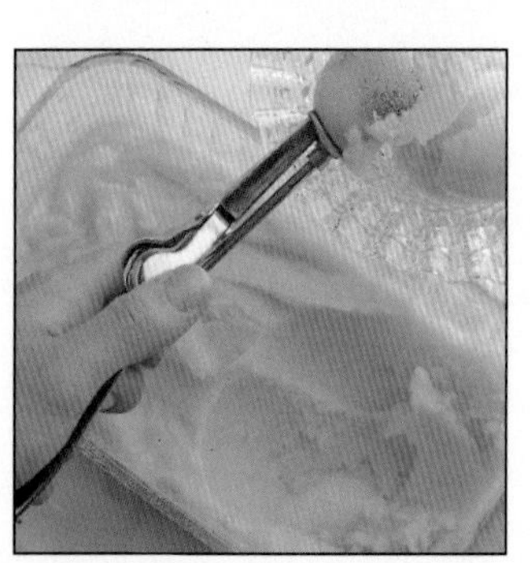

3. Serving the sorbet. Remove the sorbet from the freezer and let it soften slightly, if necessary. Serve with an ice cream scoop, dipping the utensil into a bowl of hot water if necessary to aid in scooping.

SHERBET

The sherbet recipes in this book are distinguished from sorbets by the addition of milk or yogurt and gelatin, making them both lighter and creamier. The key to achieving the desired result is fully dissolving the gelatin in water before adding it to the hot fruit mixture.

1. Dissolving the gelatin. Pour the water into a small cup or bowl. Sprinkle unflavored gelatin granules over the water and let stand until softened, about 10 minutes.

2. Combining the ingredients. Combine the fruit and sweeteners in a saucepan and cook until tender. Add the gelatin mixture and stir until dissolved. Cool until lukewarm; then purée in a food processor with the milk and corn syrup. Transfer to a bowl, cover and refrigerate until cold.

3. Freezing the sherbet. Pour the chilled sherbet mixture into an ice cream maker and process. Transfer to a freezer container and freeze until firm. Remove from the freezer and let soften slightly at room temperature if necessary to aid in scooping.

GRANITA

The Italian name *granita* refers to the granular texture of this variation on sorbet. Granitas are made without the aid of ice cream machines, using only a metal bowl, freezer, whisk and fork for the refreshingly icy result.

1. Freezing until semifirm. Pour the granita mixture into a metal bowl and freeze until semifirm, about 3 hours, whisking about every 30 minutes to promote even freezing. Then cover and freeze until solid.

2. Scraping ice crystals. Remove the bowl from the freezer and, using the tines of a table fork, firmly scrape the surface of the frozen mixture to form icy crystals. Scoop into serving dishes or glasses and serve immediately.

Lemon-Lime Granita

Finishing Touches

Most of the time, we love to eat frozen desserts just as they come, simply scooping them into bowls or onto cones. But these same recipes can be presented in even more festive ways, whether it's the homespun charm of an ice cream sandwich, the elegance of a colorful citrus container, or a scattering of sugared flowers or rainbow sprinkles.

The ideas on these pages only begin to suggest the possibilities; let your imagination lead you to others. Also, be sure to check the recipes on the following pages for still more ways to enhance your enjoyment of any frozen dessert.

Making Ice Cream Sandwiches

Use any flavor of ice cream you like for these sandwiches. Prepare or buy your favorite cookies, making sure they are of uniform size and at least 3 inches (7.5 cm) in diameter.

Filling the sandwich.
Remove ice cream from the freezer and let it soften slightly. Scoop onto the flat side of one cookie, using about ⅓ cup (3 fl oz/80 ml) for a 3-inch (7.5-cm) sandwich. Top with another cookie; press gently to spread the ice cream to the edge. Wrap airtight and freeze until firm, about 2 hours.

Sour Cream and Brown Sugar Ice Cream Sandwich

Presenting Frozen Mousses

Light and airy mousse mixtures can be frozen into a variety of shapes. Here, foil collars contain the mousse above the rim of a serving dish until it is frozen solid, giving the appearance of a risen soufflé.

1. Making a foil collar.
For each ¾-cup (6-fl oz/180-ml) ramekin, cut out a 12-by-6-inch (30-by-15-cm) piece of aluminum foil. Fold it in half lengthwise and wrap it around the ramekin, forming a collar that extends from the base to above the rim. Fold and crimp the ends to seal them. Spoon in the mousse, filling almost to the top of the foil.

2. Removing the collar.
Place the filled ramekins in the freezer and freeze until the mousse is solid. Just before serving, dip a small, thin, sharp knife blade in hot water, dry it, and run it between the mousse and collar. Then carefully unwrap the collar. Using the knife, smooth the sides of each mousse, if necessary.

Frozen Eggnog Mousse

Making and Filling Citrus Cups

To make a citrus cup, cut a 1-inch (2.5-cm) slice from the top of a citrus fruit. Cut around the pulp, then scoop it out with a small spoon. A thin slice cut from the cup's bottom will help it stand upright.

1. Filling a citrus cup.
For each cup, cut out an 8-by-1-inch (20-by-2.5-cm) strip of parchment paper or aluminum foil and form a collar inside the shell, extending it about ¾ inch (2 cm) above the rim. Secure with tape and freeze. Spoon in the mousse or softened ice cream or sorbet, filling to within ¼ inch (6 mm) of the collar's top. Freeze until solid.

2. Removing the collar.
Place the mousse-filled fruit cups in the freezer overnight. Just before serving, cut the tape. Dip a small, thin, sharp knife blade in hot water, dry it, and run it between the mousse and collar. Then carefully remove the collar, lifting it up and away from the mousse. Using the knife, smooth the sides of each mousse, if necessary.

Frozen Grand Marnier Mousse

Quick Garnishes

The three photographs below suggest just a few of the possibilities for attractive garnishes. You might also try thin shavings of chocolate, cut with a vegetable peeler; toasted nuts or coconut flakes; or whole or sliced fresh berries.

Sugared Flowers
Use only nontoxic, pesticide-free fresh flowers. Using a pastry brush, lightly brush all over with egg white. Hold the flower over a bowl of granulated sugar. Spoon over the sugar until evenly coated. Let dry for about 20 minutes before using.

Citrus Zest
Draw a citrus stripper (at left) across the surface of a clean citrus fruit to remove its zest in long strips. Zesters with tiny holes for cutting may also be used to shred the zest into thinner curls.

Store-bought Garnishes
Check the baking or ice cream sections of a well-stocked food store for a wide selection of decorations such as the chocolate jimmies, rainbow sprinkles and pastel sugar flowers shown here.

Chocolate Fudge Sauce

This rich, fudgy sauce is the perfect topping for almost any ice cream sundae. It can be prepared up to 1 week in advance, allowed to cool completely, covered and refrigerated. To reheat, place in a heavy saucepan over low heat, stirring often.

½ cup (4 fl oz/125 ml) heavy (double) cream
½ cup (4 oz/125 g) unsalted butter, cut into pieces
½ cup (4 fl oz/125 ml) light corn syrup
½ cup (2 oz/60 g) confectioners' (icing) sugar
9 oz (280 g) European bittersweet chocolate, chopped
1 teaspoon vanilla extract (essence)

In a medium-sized, heavy saucepan over medium-low heat, combine the cream, butter, corn syrup and confectioners' sugar. Stir with a wooden spatula until the butter melts and the sugar dissolves, about 3 minutes. Add the chocolate and stir over medium-low heat until melted, about 2 minutes. Remove from the heat. Stir in the vanilla and let cool slightly before using.

Makes about 2½ cups (20 fl oz/625 ml)

For mint flavor: Omit the vanilla extract and add ½ teaspoon peppermint extract (essence).

For orange flavor: Add 2 teaspoons grated orange zest along with the vanilla extract.

For mocha flavor: Add 1 tablespoon instant espresso powder dissolved in 2 teaspoons hot water along with the vanilla extract.

For raspberry flavor: Add 3 tablespoons raspberry preserves along with the vanilla extract.

Butterscotch Caramel Sauce

The sauce can be prepared up to 1 week in advance and stored, tightly covered, in the refrigerator. Reheat in a heavy saucepan over low heat, stirring often.

1 cup (7 oz/220 g) firmly packed light brown sugar
½ cup (4 fl oz/125 ml) heavy (double) cream
¼ cup (2 oz/60 g) unsalted butter, cut into pieces
2 tablespoons dark corn syrup
3 tablespoons Scotch whisky or water
1 teaspoon vanilla extract (essence)

In a medium-sized, heavy saucepan over low heat, combine the brown sugar, cream, butter, corn syrup and whisky or water. Stir with a wooden spatula until the sugar dissolves and the butter melts, about 3 minutes. Increase the heat to medium-high and bring to a boil. Continue to boil, without stirring, until the sauce thinly coats the back of a spoon or a candy thermometer registers 224°F (107°C), about 4 minutes. Remove from the heat. Stir in the vanilla and let cool slightly before using.

Makes about 1⅓ cups (11 fl oz/340 ml)

For orange flavor: Add 2 teaspoons grated orange zest along with the vanilla extract.

For coffee flavor: Add 2 teaspoons instant espresso powder along with the whisky.

For honey flavor: Omit the corn syrup and use 2 tablespoons honey in its place.

For nut caramel sauce: Add ⅓ cup (2 oz/60 g) toasted, peeled whole hazelnuts (filberts); pine nuts; pecans; walnuts or macadamia nuts along with the vanilla extract.

Chocolate Fudge Sauce

Butterscotch Caramel Sauce

Berry-Cassis Sauce

This versatile topping is great spooned over vanilla, orange, lemon or chocolate ice cream.

1 vanilla bean
1 package (1 lb/500 g) frozen unsweetened boysenberries or blackberries
⅓ cup (3 fl oz/80 ml) crème de cassis liqueur or water
¼ cup (2 oz/60 g) sugar

Place the vanilla bean on a work surface. Using a small, sharp knife, cut the bean in half lengthwise. Using the knife tip, scrape the seeds from the vanilla bean, then place the seeds and bean halves in a medium-sized, heavy saucepan. Add the frozen berries, liqueur or water and sugar and cook over medium heat, stirring occasionally, until the berries thaw and the sugar dissolves, about 15 minutes.

Increase the heat to medium-high and bring to a boil. Remove the pan from the heat, then remove the vanilla bean halves and discard. Place the mixture in a food processor fitted with the metal blade or in a blender and purée until smooth. Strain through a coarse sieve set over a large bowl to remove the seeds. Press firmly on the solids with a rubber spatula to extract as much liquid as possible; discard the solids.

Cover and refrigerate the purée until cold, at least 2 hours or for up to 2 days.

Makes about 1⅓ cups (11 fl oz/340 ml)

Berry-Cassis Sauce

Nut Crunch

An excellent addition to any ice cream that needs a little crunch. Use your favorite nut or a combination of nuts.

1 cup (4–5 oz/125–155 g) nuts such as almonds, pecans, hazelnuts (filberts), macadamia nuts, walnuts, peanuts or pistachio nuts, or a mixture
⅔ cup (5 oz/155 g) sugar
¼ cup (2 fl oz/60 ml) water
¼ cup (2 oz/60 g) unsalted butter
½ teaspoon baking soda (bicarbonate of soda)

Preheat an oven to 350°F (180°C). Spread the nuts on a baking sheet and place in the oven until lightly toasted and fragrant, about 10 minutes. Let cool, then chop coarsely. Set aside.

Grease a sheet of aluminum foil about 18 inches (50 cm) long with butter. In a medium-sized, heavy saucepan over medium-low heat, stir together the sugar, water and butter with a wooden spatula until the sugar dissolves and the butter melts, about 2 minutes. Using a pastry brush dipped in water, brush down any sugar crystals that form on the sides of the pan. Increase the heat to medium-high and boil, stirring constantly to prevent burning, until the mixture turns a caramel color, about 8 minutes.

Stir in the baking soda and then the nuts. Immediately turn the nut mixture out onto the buttered foil, separating any large clumps with the back of a spoon. Let cool completely. Transfer the nut crunch to a work surface and chop coarsely. Use immediately, or transfer to an airtight container and freeze for up to 1 month.

Makes about 2 cups (8 oz/250 g)

Nut Crunch

Peppermint Stick Ice Cream with Chocolate Fudge Sauce

3 cups (24 fl oz/750 ml) half-and-half (half cream)
¼ cup (2 fl oz/60 ml) light corn syrup
6 egg yolks
⅓ cup (5 oz/155 g) sugar
½ cup (2 oz/60 g) lightly crushed hard peppermint candies *(see note)*
¾ cup (6 fl oz/180 ml) chocolate fudge sauce *(recipe on page 14)*

The round red-and-white-striped peppermint candies called for in this recipe are available in the candy section of most supermarkets. For a special occasion, scoop the ice cream into meringue nests or shells purchased from a bakery.

Pour 2 cups (16 fl oz/500 ml) of the half-and-half and the corn syrup into a medium-sized, heavy saucepan. Bring to a simmer over medium-high heat. Remove from the heat.

In a metal bowl, whisk together the egg yolks and sugar until blended. Form a kitchen towel into a ring and place the bowl on top to prevent it from moving. Gradually pour the hot half-and-half mixture into the yolk mixture, whisking constantly. Return the mixture to the same saucepan and place over medium-low heat. Cook, stirring slowly and continuously with a wooden spatula, until the custard thickens and leaves a path on the back of the spatula when a finger is drawn across it, about 5 minutes; do not allow to boil.

Pour the custard through a medium-mesh sieve set over a clean bowl. Add half of the crushed peppermint candies and stir until melted. Add the remaining 1 cup (8 fl oz/250 ml) half-and-half and stir to combine. Refrigerate the custard until cold, about 1 hour.

Transfer the custard to an ice cream maker and process according to the manufacturer's instructions. Add the remaining candies during the final minute of processing. Transfer the ice cream to a container; cover and freeze until firm, at least 4 hours or for up to 3 days.

To serve, scoop the ice cream into 6 bowls and drizzle 2 tablespoons fudge sauce over each serving.

Makes about 4½ cups (36 fl oz/1.1 l); serves 6

Chocolate-Dipped Ice Cream Cones

- classic vanilla bean ice cream *(recipe on page 8)*
- 6 sugar cones
- 1 lb (500 g) European bittersweet chocolate, chopped
- ¼ cup (2 fl oz/60 ml) vegetable oil
- nut crunch made with nut of choice, finely chopped *(recipe on page 15)*

You can use almost any ice cream that combines well with chocolate for this scrumptious treat. Avoid using ice creams that contain wine or liqueur, as they have a softer texture than regular ice cream and would be difficult to dip. For a children's party, the dipped cones can be sprinkled with chocolate jimmies, colorful rainbow sprinkles or candied confetti, available in the baking section of food stores.

Spoon a small amount of ice cream into 1 cone, packing it gently. Dip a large ice cream scoop into hot water and scoop a large ball of ice cream onto the cone, pressing gently to adhere. Stand the cone up in a small glass and place in the freezer. Repeat with the remaining cones and ice cream, placing each in its own glass. Freeze the cones until firm, about 2 hours.

Place the chocolate and vegetable oil in a metal bowl and set over a saucepan of simmering water; do not allow the bottom of the bowl to touch the water. Stir the chocolate until melted and smooth. Remove the bowl from over the water. Let the chocolate cool slightly.

Place the nut crunch on a plate. Working quickly and tilting the bowl of chocolate, dip the ice cream end of a frozen cone into the chocolate, turning to coat evenly. Shake the cone, allowing the excess chocolate to drip back into the bowl. Immediately roll the coated ice cream in the chopped nut crunch. Stand the cone up in the small glass and return it to the freezer. Repeat with the remaining cones, chocolate and nut crunch. Freeze until the chocolate sets, about 1 hour.

Serve immediately, or wrap each cone in plastic wrap and freeze for up to 3 days.

Serves 6

Late-Harvest Riesling Ice Cream with Fresh Peaches

The large quantity of wine in this ice cream gives it a soft, silky texture. Serve the ice cream and peaches with your favorite butter cookies.

FOR THE ICE CREAM:

1½ cups (12 fl oz/375 ml) heavy (double) cream
½ cup (4 fl oz/125 ml) half-and-half (half cream)
4 egg yolks
⅔ cup (5 oz/155 g) sugar
1 cup (8 fl oz/250 ml) late-harvest Riesling wine

FOR THE PEACHES:

3 peaches, peeled, halved, pitted *(see glossary, page 107)*, and sliced
1 tablespoon late-harvest Riesling wine
1 tablespoon sugar
⅛ teaspoon crushed cardamom seeds or ground cardamom, optional

To make the ice cream, pour 1 cup (8 fl oz/250 ml) of the cream and the half-and-half into a medium-sized, heavy saucepan. Bring to a simmer over medium-high heat. Remove from the heat.

In a metal bowl, whisk together the egg yolks and sugar until blended. Form a kitchen towel into a ring and place the bowl on top to prevent it from moving. Gradually pour the hot cream mixture into the yolk mixture, whisking constantly. Return the mixture to the same saucepan and place over medium-low heat. Cook, stirring slowly and continuously with a wooden spatula, until the custard thickens and leaves a path on the back of the spatula when a finger is drawn across it, about 3 minutes; do not allow to boil.

Pour the custard through a medium-mesh sieve set over a clean bowl. Stir in the wine and the remaining ½ cup (4 fl oz/125 ml) cream. Refrigerate the custard until cold, about 1 hour.

Transfer the custard to an ice cream maker and process according to the manufacturer's instructions. Transfer the ice cream to a container; cover and freeze until firm, at least 4 hours or for up to 3 days.

To prepare the peaches, in a bowl, combine the peaches, wine, sugar and the cardamom, if using. Stir together gently and let stand for 5 minutes.

To serve, scoop the ice cream into 6 serving dishes or Riesling wine glasses. Top with the peaches and serve.

Makes about 4½ cups (36 fl oz/1.1 l) ice cream; serves 6

Cappuccino–Toffee Crunch Ice Cream

- 2¼ cups (18 fl oz/560 ml) half-and-half (half cream)
- ¼ cup (¾ oz/20 g) unsweetened cocoa
- 1 tablespoon instant espresso powder
- 1 cinnamon stick, about 3 inches (7.5 cm) long, broken in half
- 4 egg yolks
- ½ cup (4 oz/125 g) plus 1 tablespoon sugar
- 2 oz (60 g) European bittersweet chocolate, chopped
- 3 tablespoons Kahlúa or other coffee liqueur
- 1 tablespoon dark rum
- ¾ cup (3 oz/90 g) nut crunch made with almonds *(recipe on page 15)*

For heightened flavor and crunch, sprinkle additional nut crunch over scoops of the ice cream before serving.

Pour 2 cups (16 fl oz/500 ml) of the half-and-half into a medium-sized, heavy saucepan. Bring to a simmer over medium-high heat. Add the cocoa and espresso powder and whisk to blend. Add the cinnamon stick and remove from the heat.

In a metal bowl, whisk together the egg yolks and all of the sugar until blended. Form a kitchen towel into a ring and place the bowl on top to prevent it from moving. Gradually pour the hot half-and-half mixture into the yolk mixture, whisking constantly. Return the mixture to the same saucepan and place over medium-low heat. Cook, stirring slowly and continuously with a wooden spatula, until the custard thickens and leaves a path on the back of the spatula when a finger is drawn across it, about 5 minutes; do not allow to boil.

Pour the custard through a medium-mesh sieve set over a clean bowl. Add the chocolate and stir until melted. Stir in the coffee liqueur, rum and the remaining ¼ cup (2 fl oz/60 ml) half-and-half. Refrigerate the custard until cold, about 1 hour.

Transfer the custard to an ice cream maker and process according to the manufacturer's instructions. Add the nut crunch during the final minute of processing. Transfer the ice cream to a container; cover and freeze until firm, at least 4 hours or for up to 3 days.

Makes about 3½ cups (28 fl oz/875 ml); serves 4–6

Orange Ice Cream with Truffles

FOR THE TRUFFLES:
3 tablespoons sugar
2 egg yolks
⅓ cup (3 fl oz/80 ml) plus 2 tablespoons heavy (double) cream
4 oz (125 g) European bittersweet chocolate, chopped

FOR THE ICE CREAM:
2 small oranges
2 cups (16 fl oz/500 ml) heavy (double) cream
1 cup (8 fl oz/250 ml) half-and-half (half cream)
6 egg yolks
⅔ cup (5 oz/155 g) sugar
1 cup (8 fl oz/250 ml) fresh orange juice
2 teaspoons grated orange zest

To make the truffles, in a small metal bowl, whisk together the sugar and egg yolks until blended. In a small, heavy saucepan over medium-high heat, bring the ⅓ cup (3 fl oz/80 ml) cream to a simmer. Gradually whisk the hot cream into the yolk mixture. Return the mixture to the same saucepan over medium-low heat and cook, stirring continuously, until the custard thickens, about 2 minutes. Remove from the heat and stir in the chocolate until melted. Then mix in the 2 tablespoons cream. Freeze, uncovered, until firm enough to hold a shape, about 3 hours. Drop the truffle mixture by teaspoonfuls onto an aluminum foil–lined baking sheet, spacing them slightly apart. Freeze until ready to use.

To make the ice cream, using a vegetable peeler, remove the zest from the oranges in long, wide strips and place the zest in a large, heavy saucepan. Add 1 cup (8 fl oz/250 ml) of the cream and the half-and-half and bring to a simmer over medium-high heat. Remove from the heat.

In a metal bowl, whisk together the egg yolks and sugar until blended. Gradually whisk in the hot cream mixture. Return the mixture to the same saucepan and place over medium-low heat. Add the orange juice and cook, stirring continuously, until the custard thickens slightly, about 5 minutes; do not boil.

Pour the custard through a medium-mesh sieve set over a clean bowl. Stir in the remaining 1 cup (8 fl oz/250 ml) cream and the grated orange zest. Refrigerate until cold, about 1 hour.

Transfer the custard to an ice cream maker and process according to the manufacturer's instructions. Transfer half of the ice cream to a 1½–2-qt (1.5–2-l) rectangular container; top with a layer of truffles, spacing them slightly apart. Cover with the remaining ice cream. Top with more truffles in the same manner, pressing them gently into the ice cream. Cover and freeze until firm, at least 4 hours or for up to 3 days.

Makes about 5 cups (40 fl oz/1.25 l); serves 8

Strawberry Parfaits with Berry-Cassis Sauce

4 cups (1 lb/500 g) hulled fresh strawberries or frozen unsweetened strawberries, thawed
1½ cups (12 fl oz/375 ml) heavy (double) cream
¾ cup (6 oz/180 g) sugar
3 egg yolks
3 tablespoons light corn syrup

For serving:
¾ cup (6 fl oz/180 ml) berry-cassis sauce *(recipe on page 15)*
2 cups (½ lb/250 g) fresh strawberries, hulled and thinly sliced
6 fresh mint sprigs

This vibrant frozen dessert offers fresh berry flavor at its best.

In a food processor fitted with the metal blade or in a blender, place the fresh or thawed berries and any juices and purée until smooth. Pour into a large bowl and set aside. Pour 1¼ cups (10 fl oz/315 ml) of the cream into a large, heavy saucepan. Bring to a simmer over medium-high heat. Remove from the heat.

In a large metal bowl, whisk together the sugar, egg yolks, corn syrup and the remaining ¼ cup (2 fl oz/60 ml) cream until blended. Form a kitchen towel into a ring and place the bowl on top to prevent it from moving. Gradually pour the hot cream mixture into the yolk mixture, whisking constantly. Return the mixture to the same saucepan and place over medium-low heat. Cook, stirring slowly and continuously with a wooden spatula, until the custard thickens and leaves a path on the back of the spatula when a finger is drawn across it, about 5 minutes; do not allow to boil.

Pour the custard through a medium-mesh sieve into the berry purée and stir to blend. Refrigerate the custard until cold, about 1 hour.

Transfer the custard to an ice cream maker and process according to the manufacturer's instructions. Transfer the ice cream to a container; cover and freeze until firm, at least 4 hours or for up to 3 days.

To serve, scoop half of the ice cream into each of 6 parfait glasses or other serving dishes. Drizzle 1 tablespoon of berry-cassis sauce over each serving. Top with the remaining ice cream. Drizzle another 1 tablespoon sauce over each. Top with the sliced strawberries. Garnish with the mint sprigs and serve.

Makes about 4½ cups (36 fl oz/1.1 l); serves 6

Hazelnut Crunch Ice Cream

1¼ cups (6½ oz/200 g) hazelnuts (filberts)
1½ cups (12 fl oz/375 ml) whole milk
¾ cup (6 fl oz/180 ml) half-and-half (half cream)
4 egg yolks
½ cup (4 oz/125 g) sugar
¾ cup (6 fl oz/180 ml) heavy (double) cream
½ teaspoon vanilla extract (essence)
¾ cup (3 oz/90 g) nut crunch made with hazelnuts *(recipe on page 15)*
½ cup (4 fl oz/125 ml) butterscotch caramel sauce *(recipe on page 14)*

For extra crunch, sprinkle additional nut crunch over each serving.

Preheat an oven to 350°F (180°C). Spread the nuts on a baking sheet and place in the oven until toasted and fragrant, about 10 minutes. Remove from the oven and let cool. In a food processor fitted with the metal blade, finely grind the nuts; do not overprocess. Place the ground nuts in a large, heavy saucepan. Add the milk and bring to a simmer over medium-high heat. Remove from the heat. Cover and let stand for 30 minutes.

Pour the nut mixture through a coarse sieve into a heavy saucepan, pressing firmly on the solids with a rubber spatula to extract as much liquid as possible. Stir in the half-and-half. Bring to a simmer over medium-high heat. Remove from the heat. In a metal bowl, whisk together the egg yolks and sugar until blended. Form a kitchen towel into a ring and place the bowl on top to prevent it from moving. Gradually pour the hot milk mixture into the yolk mixture, whisking constantly. Return the mixture to the same saucepan and place over medium-low heat. Cook, stirring slowly and continuously with a wooden spatula, until the custard thickens and leaves a path on the back of the spatula when a finger is drawn across it, about 6 minutes; do not allow to boil.

Pour the custard through the coarse sieve into a clean bowl. Stir in the cream and vanilla; refrigerate until cold, about 1 hour.

Transfer the custard to an ice cream maker and process according to the manufacturer's instructions. Add the nut crunch during the final minute. Transfer to a container; cover and freeze until firm, at least 4 hours or for up to 3 days.

To serve, scoop the ice cream into 4 serving dishes. Drizzle 2 tablespoons sauce over each serving.

Makes about 3 cups (24 fl oz/750 ml); serves 4

Belgian White Chocolate Ice Cream

- 4 cups (32 fl oz/1 l) half-and-half (half cream)
- 6 egg yolks
- ½ cup (4 oz/125 g) sugar
- 6 oz (185 g) European white chocolate, chopped *(see note)*

White chocolate purists will love this elegant ice cream on its own. Look for Lindt, Callebaut or other high-quality European white chocolate for the finest flavor. For an added embellishment, try it drizzled with berry-cassis sauce (recipe on page 15) or chocolate fudge sauce (page 14).

Pour 3 cups (24 fl oz/750 ml) of the half-and-half into a large, heavy saucepan. Bring to a simmer over medium-high heat. Remove from the heat.

In a metal bowl, whisk together the egg yolks and sugar until blended. Form a kitchen towel into a ring and place the bowl on top to prevent it from moving. Gradually pour the hot half-and-half into the yolk mixture, whisking constantly. Return the mixture to the same saucepan and place over medium-low heat. Cook, stirring slowly and continuously with a wooden spatula, until the custard thickens and leaves a path on the back of the spatula when a finger is drawn across it, about 5 minutes; do not allow to boil.

Pour the custard through a medium-mesh sieve set over a clean bowl. Add the chocolate and stir until melted. Stir in the remaining 1 cup (8 fl oz/250 ml) half-and-half. Refrigerate the custard until cold, about 1 hour.

Transfer the custard to an ice cream maker and process according to the manufacturer's instructions. Transfer the ice cream to a container; cover and freeze until firm, at least 4 hours or for up to 3 days.

Makes about 6 cups (48 fl oz/1.5 l); serves 8–10

Boysenberry Ice Cream

4 cups (1 lb/500 g) fresh boysenberries or frozen unsweetened boysenberries, thawed
1½ cups (12 fl oz/375 ml) heavy (double) cream
¾ cup (6 oz/185 g) sugar
3 egg yolks

This beautiful fuschia-colored ice cream is delicious on its own or as an à la mode topping for your favorite berry cobbler or pie.

In a food processor fitted with the metal blade or in a blender, place the fresh or thawed berries and any juices and purée until smooth. Set aside. Pour 1¼ cups (10 fl oz/315 ml) of the cream into a large, heavy saucepan. Bring to a simmer over medium-high heat. Remove from the heat.

In a large metal bowl, whisk together the sugar, egg yolks and the remaining ¼ cup (2 fl oz/60 ml) cream until blended. Form a kitchen towel into a ring and place the bowl on top to prevent it from moving. Gradually pour the hot cream into the yolk mixture, whisking constantly. Return the mixture to the same saucepan and place over medium-low heat. Cook, stirring slowly and continuously with a wooden spatula, until the custard thickens and leaves a path on the back of the spatula when a finger is drawn across it, about 5 minutes; do not allow to boil. Remove from the heat. Add the berry purée to the custard and stir to blend.

Pour the custard through a coarse sieve set over a clean large bowl to remove the seeds. Press firmly on the solids with a rubber spatula to extract as much liquid as possible; discard the solids. Refrigerate the custard until cold, about 1 hour.

Transfer the custard to an ice cream maker and process according to the manufacturer's instructions. Transfer the ice cream to a container; cover and freeze until firm, at least 4 hours or for up to 3 days.

Makes about 4½ cups (36 fl oz/1.1 l); serves 6–8

Pear-Walnut Ice Cream Sundaes

1 lb (500 g) very ripe pears such as Bartlett or Comice, peeled, quartered and cored
½ cup (4 fl oz/125 ml) canned pear nectar
6 tablespoons (3 oz/90 g) sugar
1 cup (8 fl oz/250 ml) heavy (double) cream
3 egg yolks
2 tablespoons light corn syrup
½ teaspoon vanilla extract (essence)
⅔ cup (2½ oz/75 g) walnut halves
½ cup (4 fl oz/125 ml) butterscotch caramel sauce *(recipe on page 14)*

For an elegant dessert, top the ice cream with sautéed pear slices.

In a heavy saucepan over medium-high heat, combine the pears, nectar and 3 tablespoons of the sugar. Stir until the pear mixture begins to boil, about 3 minutes. Boil for 1 minute longer. Remove from the heat. In a food processor fitted with the metal blade or in a blender, purée the pears. Set aside.

Pour the cream into a large, heavy saucepan. Bring to a simmer over medium-high heat. Remove from the heat.

In a metal bowl, whisk together the egg yolks, corn syrup and the remaining 3 tablespoons sugar until blended. Form a kitchen towel into a ring and place the bowl on top to prevent it from moving. Gradually pour the hot cream into the yolk mixture, whisking constantly. Return the mixture to the same saucepan and place over medium-low heat. Cook, stirring slowly and continuously with a wooden spatula, until the custard thickens and leaves a path on the back of the spatula when a finger is drawn across it, about 3 minutes; do not allow to boil.

Pour the custard through a medium-mesh sieve set over a clean bowl. Stir in the pear purée and the vanilla. Refrigerate the custard until cold, about 1 hour.

Preheat an oven to 350°F (180°C). Spread the nuts on a baking sheet and place in the oven until lightly toasted and fragrant, about 10 minutes. Let cool, then chop coarsely; set aside.

Transfer the custard to an ice cream maker and process according to the manufacturer's instructions. Add the walnuts during the final minute. Transfer to a container; cover and freeze until firm, at least 4 hours or for up to 3 days.

To serve, scoop the ice cream into 4 bowls. Drizzle 2 tablespoons sauce over each serving.

Makes about 3¼ cups (26 fl oz/810 ml); serves 4

Chocolate Ice Cream with Fudge Swirl

- 2 cups (16 fl oz/500 ml) half-and-half (half cream)
- 3 egg yolks
- ½ cup (4 oz/125 g) sugar
- 2 tablespoons light corn syrup
- 5 oz (155 g) European bittersweet chocolate, chopped
- ½ teaspoon vanilla extract (essence)
- 4 tablespoons chocolate fudge sauce, cooled to lukewarm *(recipe on page 14)*

For a pretty presentation, garnish scoops of the ice cream with sugared edible flowers or rose petals (see page 13).

Pour 1½ cups (12 fl oz/375 ml) of the half-and-half into a medium-sized, heavy saucepan. Bring to a simmer over medium-high heat. Remove from the heat.

In a metal bowl, whisk together the egg yolks, sugar and corn syrup until blended. Form a kitchen towel into a ring and place the bowl on top to prevent it from moving. Gradually add the hot half-and-half, whisking constantly. Return the mixture to the same saucepan and place over medium-low heat. Cook, stirring slowly and continuously with a wooden spatula, until the custard thickens and leaves a path on the back of the spatula when a finger is drawn across it, about 5 minutes; do not allow to boil.

Pour the custard through a medium-mesh sieve into a clean bowl. Add the chocolate and stir until melted. Stir in the vanilla and the remaining ½ cup (4 fl oz/125 ml) half-and-half. Refrigerate the custard until cold, about 1 hour.

Transfer the custard to an ice cream maker and process according to the manufacturer's instructions. Transfer half of the ice cream to a 1½-qt (1.5-l) rectangular container. Drizzle 2 tablespoons of the fudge sauce over the ice cream. Top with the remaining ice cream, smoothing the top gently. Drizzle the remaining 2 tablespoons fudge sauce over the ice cream. Cover and freeze until firm, at least 4 hours or for up to 3 days.

Makes about 3½ cups (28 fl oz/875 ml); serves 4–6

Lemon Ice Cream with Lemon-Ginger Sauce

FOR THE ICE CREAM:

2 cups (16 fl oz/500 ml) half-and-half (half cream)

2 cups (16 fl oz/500 ml) heavy (double) cream

6 egg yolks

1¼ cups (10 oz/315 g) granulated sugar

1 tablespoon grated lemon zest

¾ cup (6 fl oz/180 ml) fresh lemon juice

FOR THE SAUCE:

½ cup (4 oz/125 g) granulated sugar

½ cup (3½ oz/105 g) firmly packed golden brown sugar

⅓ cup (3 fl oz/80 ml) water

¼ cup (2 fl oz/60 ml) fresh lemon juice

3 tablespoons unsalted butter

1 teaspoon grated lemon zest

2 tablespoons minced crystallized ginger

Lemon lovers will delight in this tangy citrus ice cream.

To make the ice cream, pour the half-and-half and 1 cup (8 fl oz/250 ml) of the cream into a large, heavy saucepan. Bring to a simmer over medium-high heat. Remove from the heat.

In a large metal bowl, whisk together the egg yolks, granulated sugar and lemon zest until blended. Form a kitchen towel into a ring and place the bowl on top to prevent it from moving. Gradually pour the hot half-and-half mixture into the yolk mixture, whisking constantly. Return the mixture to the same saucepan and place over medium-low heat. Cook, stirring slowly and continuously with a wooden spatula, until the custard thickens and leaves a path on the back of the spatula when a finger is drawn across it, about 5 minutes; do not allow to boil.

Pour the custard into a clean bowl; do not strain. Whisk in the lemon juice and the remaining 1 cup (8 fl oz/250 ml) cream. Refrigerate the custard until cold, about 1 hour.

Transfer the custard to an ice cream maker and process according to the manufacturer's instructions. Transfer the ice cream to a container; cover and freeze until firm, at least 4 hours or for up to 3 days.

To make the sauce, in a heavy saucepan over medium heat, combine the sugars, water, lemon juice, butter and lemon zest. Stir until the sugars dissolve, about 3 minutes. Simmer, stirring occasionally, until reduced to 1 cup (8 fl oz/250 ml), about 15 minutes. Remove from the heat. Let cool. Stir in the ginger.

To serve, scoop the ice cream into 8 balloon-shaped wine glasses. Drizzle 1–2 tablespoons sauce over each serving.

Makes about 6 cups (48 fl oz/1.5 l) ice cream; serves 8

Prune and Armagnac Ice Cream

- 1 cup (6 oz/185 g) coarsely chopped pitted prunes
- ¾ cup (6 fl oz/180 ml) Armagnac or Cognac
- 3 cups (24 fl oz/750 ml) half-and-half (half cream)
- 6 egg yolks
- 1 cup (8 oz/250 g) sugar
- 1 cup (8 fl oz/250 ml) heavy (double) cream
- 2 teaspoons vanilla extract (essence)

Armagnac, a French brandy produced primarily southeast of Bordeaux, is known for its pungent fragrance and smooth flavor. It is often paired with prunes in French desserts, a marriage that works particularly well in ice cream. The high proportion of Armagnac in the custard gives this ice cream its soft texture.

In a small bowl, combine the prunes and ½ cup (4 fl oz/120 ml) of the Armagnac. Let stand until the prunes absorb almost all of the liquid, about 3 hours.

Pour the half-and-half into a medium-sized, heavy saucepan. Bring to a simmer over medium-high heat. Remove from the heat.

In a metal bowl, whisk together the egg yolks and sugar until blended. Form a kitchen towel into a ring and place the bowl on top to prevent it from moving. Gradually pour the hot half-and-half into the yolk mixture, whisking constantly. Return the mixture to the same saucepan and place over medium-low heat. Cook, stirring slowly and continuously with a wooden spatula, until the custard thickens and leaves a path on the back of the spatula when a finger is drawn across it, about 5 minutes; do not allow to boil.

Pour the custard through a medium-mesh sieve into a clean bowl. Stir in the cream, vanilla and the remaining ¼ cup (2 fl oz/60 ml) Armagnac. Refrigerate the custard until cold, about 1 hour.

Transfer the custard to an ice cream maker and process according to the manufacturer's instructions. Add the prunes during the final minute of processing. Transfer the ice cream to a container; cover and freeze until firm, at least 4 hours or for up to 3 days.

Makes about 6 cups (48 fl oz/1.5 l); serves 8–10

Sour Cream and Brown Sugar Ice Cream

- 2 cups (16 fl oz/500 ml) half-and-half (half cream)
- 6 egg yolks
- 1 cup (7 oz/220 g) firmly packed golden brown sugar
- 3 tablespoons dark corn syrup
- 2 cups (16 fl oz/500 ml) sour cream
- 1 teaspoon vanilla extract (essence)

Serve this luscious ice cream topped with sliced ripe peaches that have been macerated with a little sugar. Or, for a special children's treat, make ice cream sandwiches by pressing ⅓ cup (3 fl oz/80 ml) of the ice cream between two large chocolate-chip or gingersnap cookies. Wrap the sandwiches airtight and freeze until firm, about 2 hours.

Pour the half-and-half into a large, heavy saucepan. Bring to a simmer over medium-high heat. Remove from the heat.

In a large metal bowl, whisk together the egg yolks, brown sugar and corn syrup until blended. Form a kitchen towel into a ring and place the bowl on top to prevent it from moving. Gradually pour the hot half-and-half into the yolk mixture, whisking constantly. Return the mixture to the same saucepan and place over medium-low heat. Cook, stirring slowly and continuously with a wooden spatula, until the custard thickens and leaves a path on the back of the spatula when a finger is drawn across it, about 5 minutes; do not allow to boil.

Pour the custard through a medium-mesh sieve set over a clean bowl. Add the sour cream and vanilla and whisk until smooth. Refrigerate the custard until cold, about 1 hour.

Transfer the custard to an ice cream maker and process according to the manufacturer's instructions. Transfer the ice cream to a container; cover and freeze until firm, at least 4 hours or for up to 3 days.

Makes about 5 cups (40 fl oz/1.25 l); serves 8

Coconut Ice Cream

- 1¼ cups (5 oz/155 g) packed sweetened flaked coconut
- 1½ cups (12 fl oz/375 ml) half-and-half (half cream)
- ¾ cup (6 fl oz/180 ml) canned sweetened cream of coconut
- 6 egg yolks
- ⅓ cup (3 oz/90 g) sugar
- 1½ cups (12 fl oz/375 ml) heavy (double) cream

For a double coconut treat, stir ½ cup (1½ oz/45 g) toasted shredded coconut into the ice cream during the final minute of processing. To make a colorful sundae, garnish the ice cream with diced tropical fruit.

In a large, heavy saucepan over medium-high heat, place the flaked coconut. Stir the coconut until it begins to brown, about 7 minutes. Add the half-and-half and bring to a simmer. Remove from the heat. Cover and let stand for 30 minutes.

Pour the coconut mixture through a medium-mesh sieve set over a large bowl, pressing on the coconut with a rubber spatula to extract as much liquid as possible; discard the coconut. Return the coconut milk to the same saucepan and place over medium-high heat. Add the cream of coconut and bring to a simmer. Remove from the heat.

In a metal bowl, whisk together the egg yolks and sugar until blended. Form a kitchen towel into a ring and place the bowl on top to prevent it from moving. Gradually pour the hot coconut-milk mixture into the yolk mixture, whisking constantly. Return the mixture to the same saucepan and place over medium-low heat. Cook, stirring slowly and continuously with a wooden spatula, until the custard thickens and leaves a path on the back of the spatula when a finger is drawn across it, about 5 minutes; do not allow to boil.

Pour the custard through the medium-mesh sieve set over a clean bowl. Add the cream and stir well. Refrigerate the custard until cold, about 1 hour.

Transfer the custard to an ice cream maker and process according to the manufacturer's instructions. Transfer the ice cream to a container; cover and freeze until firm, at least 4 hours or for up to 3 days.

Makes about 4½ cups (36 fl oz/1.1 l); serves 6–8

Holiday Pumpkin Spice Ice Cream

- 2 cups (16 fl oz/500 ml) heavy (double) cream
- ⅔ cup (5 oz/155 g) sugar
- ½ cup (4 fl oz/125 ml) light corn syrup
- 6 egg yolks
- 1 teaspoon ground ginger
- ½ teaspoon ground cinnamon
- ¼ teaspoon freshly grated nutmeg
- ⅔ cup (5 oz/155 g) canned solid-pack pumpkin
- 1 teaspoon vanilla extract (essence)

This rich and creamy ice cream is perfect for the holiday season. Try it served atop a slice of homemade apple or pecan pie.

Pour 1⅓ cups (11 fl oz/340 ml) of the cream into a medium-sized, heavy saucepan. Bring to a simmer over medium-high heat. Remove from the heat.

In a metal bowl, whisk together the sugar, corn syrup, egg yolks, ginger, cinnamon and nutmeg until blended. Form a kitchen towel into a ring and place the bowl on top to prevent it from moving. Gradually pour the hot cream into the yolk mixture, whisking constantly. Return the mixture to the same saucepan and place over medium-low heat. Cook, stirring slowly and continuously with a wooden spatula, until the custard thickens and leaves a path on the back of the spatula when a finger is drawn across it, about 5 minutes; do not allow to boil.

Pour the custard through a medium-mesh sieve set over a clean bowl. Add the pumpkin, vanilla and the remaining ⅔ cup (5 fl oz/160 ml) cream and whisk until blended. Refrigerate the custard until cold, about 1 hour.

Transfer the custard to an ice cream maker and process according to the manufacturer's instructions. Transfer the ice cream to a container; cover and freeze until firm, at least 4 hours or for up to 3 days.

Makes about 4 cups (32 fl oz/1 l); serves 6

Toasted Almond Ice Cream

2 tablespoons unsalted butter
½ cup (2½ oz/75 g) coarsely chopped almonds
3 cups (24 fl oz/750 ml) half-and-half (half cream)
6 egg yolks
¾ cup (6 oz/185 g) sugar
2 tablespoons light corn syrup
1 teaspoon vanilla extract (essence)
½ teaspoon almond extract (essence)

Sautéing the almonds in butter intensifies the flavor of this simple ice cream. You determine the texture: strain out the almonds for smooth, leave them in for crunchy. Offer almond macaroon cookies as an accompaniment to either variety.

In a large, heavy saucepan over medium-high heat, melt the butter. Add the almonds and sauté, stirring often, until the almonds are golden and the butter browns, about 5 minutes; do not burn. Add the half-and-half and bring to a simmer. Remove from the heat.

In a metal bowl, whisk together the egg yolks, sugar and corn syrup until blended. Form a kitchen towel into a ring and place the bowl on top to prevent it from moving. Gradually pour the hot half-and-half mixture into the yolk mixture, whisking constantly. Return the mixture to the same saucepan and place over medium-low heat. Cook, stirring slowly and continuously with a wooden spatula, until the custard thickens and leaves a path on the back of the spatula when a finger is drawn across it, about 5 minutes; do not allow to boil.

Pour the custard through a medium-mesh sieve into a clean bowl for a smooth texture, or do not strain for a crunchy texture. Stir in the vanilla and almond extracts. Refrigerate the custard until cold, about 1 hour.

Transfer the custard to an ice cream maker and process according to the manufacturer's instructions. Transfer the ice cream to a container; cover and freeze until firm, at least 4 hours or for up to 3 days.

Makes about 5 cups (40 fl oz/1.25 l); serves 8

Fresh Peach Ice Cream

- 2 cups (12 oz/375 g) peeled and finely chopped ripe peaches *(see glossary, page 107)*
- ½ cup (4 oz/120 g) sugar
- ¼ cup (2 fl oz/60 ml) light corn syrup
- 1½ cups (12 fl oz/375 ml) half-and-half (half cream)
- 1 cup (8 fl oz/250 ml) heavy (double) cream
- 4 egg yolks
- ½ teaspoon vanilla extract (essence)

For the best possible flavor, use only the ripest, juiciest peaches for this summertime treat.

Place the peaches in a large, heavy saucepan. Add ¼ cup (2 oz/60 g) of the sugar and the corn syrup and place over medium heat. Stir until the sugar melts and the peaches are heated through, about 4 minutes. Pour into a large bowl and set aside. Add the half-and-half and ½ cup (4 fl oz/125 ml) of the cream to the same saucepan. Bring to a simmer over medium-high heat. Remove from the heat.

In a metal bowl, whisk together the egg yolks and the remaining ¼ cup (2 oz/60 g) sugar until blended. Form a kitchen towel into a ring and place the bowl on top to prevent it from moving. Gradually pour the hot half-and-half mixture into the yolk mixture, whisking constantly. Return the mixture to the saucepan and place over medium-low heat. Cook, stirring slowly and continuously with a wooden spatula, until the custard thickens and leaves a path on the back of the spatula when a finger is drawn across it, about 5 minutes; do not allow to boil.

Pour the custard through a medium-mesh sieve into the peach mixture. Transfer three-fourths of the peach mixture to a food processor fitted with the metal blade or to a blender and purée until smooth. Pour the purée back into the remaining peach mixture. Add the vanilla and remaining ½ cup (4 fl oz/125 ml) cream and whisk to blend. Refrigerate until cold, about 1 hour.

Transfer the peach mixture to an ice cream maker and process according to the manufacturer's instructions. Transfer the ice cream to a container; cover and freeze until firm, at least 4 hours or for up to 3 days.

Makes about 5 cups (40 fl oz/1.25 l); serves 8

Frozen Tiramisù Cake

Mascarpone, an Italian triple cream cheese, is available at Italian markets and some specialty-food stores.

- 1½ cups (12 oz/375 g) sugar
- ¾ cup (6 fl oz/180 ml) water
- 2 tablespoons instant espresso powder
- ⅓ cup (3 fl oz/80 ml) Kahlúa or other coffee-flavored liqueur
- 8 egg yolks
- 6 tablespoons (3 fl oz/90 ml) sweet Marsala wine
- 1 lb (500 g) mascarpone cheese
- ½ cup (4 fl oz/125 ml) heavy (double) cream
- 1 teaspoon vanilla extract (essence)
- 1 store-bought pound cake, ¾ lb (375 g), cut crosswise into slices ¼ inch (6 mm) thick
- unsweetened cocoa

In a small, heavy saucepan over low heat, combine ½ cup (4 oz/125 g) of the sugar, ½ cup (4 fl oz/120 ml) of the water and the espresso powder. Stir until the sugar dissolves, about 3 minutes. Stir in the liqueur. Remove from the heat and set aside to cool.

In a large metal bowl, whisk together the egg yolks, Marsala and the remaining 1 cup (8 oz/250 g) sugar and ¼ cup (2 fl oz/60 ml) water until blended. Set the bowl over a saucepan of simmering water; do not allow the bowl to touch the water. Whisk constantly until a candy thermometer registers 165°F (74°C), about 6 minutes. Remove the bowl from over the water.

Using an electric mixer set on high speed, beat the yolk mixture until cool and thick, about 5 minutes. In another large bowl, whisk together the mascarpone, cream and vanilla just until blended. Beat in the yolk mixture just until combined.

Select a springform pan 9 inches (23 cm) in diameter and 3 inches (7.5 cm) deep. Arrange enough of the cake slices in a single layer on the bottom of the pan to cover completely, trimming to fit as necessary. Brush half of the sugar syrup over the cake slices and then pour in half of the cheese mixture. Top with enough of the remaining cake slices to cover in a single layer, again trimming to fit. Brush the slices with the remaining syrup. Pour the remaining cheese mixture over the top, then smooth with a rubber spatula. Cover and freeze overnight.

Run a small, sharp knife around the pan sides to loosen the cake. Release the pan sides and carefully transfer the cake to a platter. Using a sifter or fine-mesh sieve, dust the top lightly with cocoa. Cut into wedges and serve immediately.

Serves 12

Frozen Lime Parfaits with Berry-Cassis Sauce

⅔ cup (5 oz/155 g) sugar
¼ cup (2 fl oz/60 ml) fresh lime juice
4 egg yolks
2 tablespoons light corn syrup
½ teaspoon grated lime zest
1 cup (8 fl oz/250 ml) heavy (double) cream, chilled
¾ cup (6 fl oz/180 ml) berry-cassis sauce *(recipe on page 15)*

The refreshing flavor and vibrant colors of this elegant dessert make it a perfect finale to any spring or summer meal.

In a large metal bowl, whisk together the sugar, lime juice, egg yolks, corn syrup and lime zest until blended. Set the bowl over a large saucepan of simmering water; do not allow the bottom of the bowl to touch the water. Whisk constantly until a candy thermometer registers 170°F (77°C), about 10 minutes.

Remove the bowl from over the water and, using an electric mixer set on high speed, beat the egg yolk mixture until cool and thick, about 6 minutes.

Place the cream in a bowl. Using the electric mixer fitted with clean, dry beaters, beat the cream on medium-high speed until stiff peaks form. Using a rubber spatula, fold the cream into the cooled yolk mixture until no white streaks remain. Transfer the mousse to a container; cover and freeze until firm, at least 8 hours or for up to 3 days.

To serve, scoop half of the lime mousse into each of 6 serving dishes. Drizzle 1 tablespoon sauce over each serving. Top with the remaining mousse and then drizzle each with another 1 tablespoon sauce. Serve immediately.

Makes about 4 cups (32 fl oz/1 l) mousse; serves 6

Frozen Grand Marnier Mousse

- 8 large thick-skinned navel oranges
- 6 egg yolks
- 1 cup (8 oz/250 g) sugar
- ½ cup (4 fl oz/125 ml) fresh orange juice
- ⅓ cup (3 fl oz/80 ml) Grand Marnier or other orange-flavored liqueur
- 2 cups (16 fl oz/500 ml) heavy (double) cream, chilled
- 1 teaspoon grated orange zest

You will impress your guests by serving this easy mousse in frozen hollowed-out oranges. To make this dessert ahead, simply wrap the frozen mousse in the orange shell in plastic wrap and freeze for up to 1 week before serving.

Following the directions on page 13 for making and filling citrus cups, hollow out the oranges. Place the orange cups upright on an aluminum foil–lined baking sheet. Form the collars as directed and place the baking sheet in a freezer.

In a large metal bowl, whisk together the egg yolks, sugar and orange juice until blended. Set the bowl over a saucepan of simmering water; do not allow the bottom of the bowl to touch the water. Whisk constantly until a candy thermometer registers 170°F (77°C), about 10 minutes.

Remove the bowl from over the water and, using an electric mixer set on high speed, beat the yolk mixture until cool and thick, about 6 minutes. Beat in the liqueur.

In a bowl, combine the cream and orange zest. Using the electric mixer fitted with clean, dry beaters, beat the orange cream on medium-high speed until stiff peaks form. Using a rubber spatula, fold the orange cream into the cooled yolk mixture. Spoon the mixture into the prepared orange cups, dividing it equally. Freeze uncovered overnight.

To remove the parchment paper or aluminum foil, cut the collars along the taped edge. Run hot water over a knife blade, wipe dry and run the blade between the mousse and collar. Carefully remove the collar, lifting it up and away from the mousse. Smooth the sides of each mousse with the knife, if necessary. Serve the oranges in doily-lined serving dishes.

Serves 8

Frozen Lemon Mousse with Blueberries

8 egg yolks
1 cup (8 oz/250 g) sugar
⅔ cup (5 fl oz/160 ml) fresh lemon juice
¼ cup (2 fl oz/60 ml) light corn syrup
2 teaspoons grated lemon zest
2 cups (16 fl oz/500 ml) heavy (double) cream, chilled
½ cup (5 oz/155 g) seedless raspberry jam
4 cups (1 lb/500 g) blueberries
fresh mint sprigs

Offer this lemony dessert the next time you are planning a summertime party. It can be made up to 3 days in advance.

Line a 2-qt (2-l) ring mold or bundt pan with plastic wrap, overhanging the edges by about 3 inches (7.5 cm). Set aside.

In a large metal bowl, whisk together the egg yolks, sugar, lemon juice, corn syrup and lemon zest until blended. Set the bowl over a large saucepan of simmering water; do not allow the bottom of the bowl to touch the water. Whisk constantly until a candy thermometer registers 170°F (77°C), about 10 minutes.

Remove the bowl from over the water and, using an electric mixer set on high speed, beat the yolk mixture until cool and thick, about 6 minutes.

Place the cream in a bowl. Using the electric mixer fitted with clean, dry beaters, beat the cream at medium-high speed until stiff peaks form. Using a rubber spatula, fold the cream into the cooled yolk mixture until no white streaks remain. Spoon into the prepared pan. Cover and freeze overnight or for up to 3 days.

About 1 hour before serving, place a round platter in the freezer. In a large, heavy frying pan over medium heat, stir the jam just until melted. Remove the pan from the heat and add the blueberries. Toss the berries to coat them thinly with the jam. Let cool completely, about 1 hour.

Uncover the mousse. Invert the pan onto the frozen platter. Lift off the pan and peel off the plastic wrap. Spoon enough of the blueberries into the center of the ring to fill nicely. Garnish with mint sprigs and serve. Pass the remaining berries separately.

Serves 10–12

Frozen Marsala Zabaglione with Strawberries

½ cup (4 fl oz/125 ml) sweet Marsala wine
½ cup (4 oz/125 g) plus 3 tablespoons sugar
5 egg yolks
1 cup (8 fl oz/250 ml) heavy (double) cream, chilled
6 cups (1½ lb/750 g) fresh strawberries, hulled and sliced

Marsala, a sherrylike fortified wine from Sicily, adds distinctive flavor to this dessert. If you prefer the zabaglione to have a crunchy texture, fold ⅔ cup (2 oz/60 g) lightly crushed amaretto cookies into the mixture just before filling the mold.

Line an 8½-by-4½-by-2½-inch (22-by-12-by-6-cm) metal loaf pan with plastic wrap, overhanging the edges by about 3 inches (7.5 cm). Place the pan in the freezer.

In a large metal bowl, whisk together the Marsala, the ½ cup (4 oz/125 g) sugar and the egg yolks until blended. Set the bowl over a saucepan of simmering water; do not allow the bottom of the bowl to touch the water. Whisk constantly until a candy thermometer registers 170°F (77°C), about 5 minutes.

Remove the bowl from over the water and, using an electric mixer set on high speed, beat the egg yolk mixture until cool and thick, about 5 minutes.

Place the cream in a bowl. Using the electric mixer fitted with clean, dry beaters, beat the cream on medium-high speed until stiff peaks form. Using a rubber spatula, fold the cream into the cooled yolk mixture until no white streaks remain. Pour into the prepared pan. Cover and freeze overnight.

About 1 hour before serving, place a platter in the freezer. Just before serving, in a bowl, toss the strawberries with the remaining 3 tablespoons sugar. Let stand for 10 minutes.

Uncover the zabaglione. Invert the pan onto the frozen platter. Lift off the pan and peel off the plastic wrap. Using a long, sharp knife, cut the mold crosswise into 10 equal slices and transfer to plates. Spoon the strawberries over the top and serve at once.

Serves 10

Frozen Eggnog Mousse

- 6 egg yolks
- 1 cup (8 oz/250 g) sugar
- ¼ cup (2 fl oz/60 ml) water
- 2 cups (16 fl oz/500 ml) heavy (double) cream, chilled
- 3 tablespoons dark rum
- 3 tablespoons brandy
- 1½ teaspoons vanilla extract (essence)
- ¼ teaspoon freshly grated nutmeg, plus extra for garnish

Frozen in individual soufflé dishes, these rich desserts are a lovely finale to a formal Christmas dinner. They are an especially good choice when you want to make your dessert ahead of time, as they can be stored in the freezer for up to 1 week.

Following the directions on page 12 for presenting frozen mousses, wrap foil collars around the outside of each of six ¾-cup (6-fl oz/180-ml) ramekins. Set aside.

In a metal bowl, whisk together the egg yolks, sugar and water until blended. Set the bowl over a saucepan of simmering water; do not allow the bottom of the bowl to touch the water. Whisk constantly until a candy thermometer registers 170°F (77°C), about 10 minutes.

Remove the bowl from over the water and, using an electric mixer set on high speed, beat the yolk mixture until cool and thick, about 6 minutes.

In a large bowl, combine the cream, rum, brandy, vanilla and the ¼ teaspoon nutmeg. Using the electric mixer fitted with clean, dry beaters, beat on medium-high speed until stiff peaks form. Using a rubber spatula, fold the cream into the cooled yolk mixture until no white streaks remain. Spoon into the prepared ramekins, dividing it equally. Freeze uncovered overnight.

Carefully unwrap the foil collars from the dishes, using a small, sharp knife as an aid, if necessary. Smooth the sides of the mousses with the knife, if necessary. Sprinkle with additional nutmeg and serve immediately.

Serves 6

Dark Chocolate Gelato

- 2 cups (16 fl oz/500 ml) whole milk
- 5 egg yolks
- ¾ cup (6 oz/185 g) sugar
- 2 tablespoons light corn syrup
- 4 oz (125 g) European bittersweet chocolate, chopped
- ¼ cup (¾ oz/20 g) unsweetened cocoa

Serve this gelato right out of the machine to highlight its ultra-creamy texture.

Pour the milk into a medium-sized, heavy saucepan. Bring to a simmer over medium-high heat. Remove from the heat.

In a metal bowl, whisk together the egg yolks, sugar and corn syrup until blended. Form a kitchen towel into a ring and place the bowl on top to prevent it from moving. Gradually pour the hot milk into the yolk mixture, whisking constantly. Return the mixture to the same saucepan and place over medium-low heat. Cook, stirring slowly and continuously with a wooden spatula, until the custard thickens and leaves a path on the back of the spatula when a finger is drawn across it, about 6 minutes; do not allow to boil.

Pour the custard through a medium-mesh sieve set over a clean metal bowl. Add the chocolate and cocoa and stir until the chocolate melts. Refrigerate until cold, about 1 hour.

Transfer the custard to an ice cream maker and process according to the manufacturer's instructions. For the best texture, serve the gelato immediately. Or transfer to a container, cover and freeze until firm, at least 4 hours or for up to 3 days. (Note: the longer freezing results in a texture more like that of ice cream.)

Makes about 4 cups (32 fl oz/1 l); serves 6

Citrus Gelato

2 oranges
2 lemons
3 cups (24 fl oz/750 ml) whole milk
8 egg yolks
1 cup (8 oz/250 g) sugar
3 tablespoons light corn syrup

Lovely fresh citrus gives this gelato its distinctive flavor. Garnish each serving simply with fresh mint sprigs and citrus zest curls, or serve small scoops of the gelato in frozen hollowed-out orange halves.

Using a vegetable peeler, remove the zest from the oranges and lemons in strips. Place the strips in a medium-sized, heavy saucepan and add the milk. Bring to a simmer over medium-high heat. Remove from the heat.

In a metal bowl, whisk together the egg yolks, sugar and corn syrup until blended. Form a kitchen towel into a ring and place the bowl on top to prevent it from moving. Gradually pour the hot milk mixture into the yolk mixture, whisking constantly. Return the mixture to the same saucepan and place over medium-low heat. Cook, stirring slowly and continuously with a wooden spatula, until the custard thickens and leaves a path on the back of the spatula when a finger is drawn across it, about 6 minutes; do not allow to boil.

Pour the custard through a medium-mesh sieve set over a clean bowl. Refrigerate until cold, about 1 hour.

Transfer the custard to an ice cream maker and process according to the manufacturer's instructions. For the best texture, serve the gelato immediately. Or transfer to a container, cover and freeze until firm, at least 4 hours or for up to 3 days. (Note: the longer freezing results in a texture more like that of ice cream.)

Makes about 3¾ cups (30 fl oz/940 ml); serves 4–6

Caramel Gelato

¾ cup (6 oz/185 g) sugar
¼ cup (2 fl oz/60 ml) water
2 cups (16 fl oz/500 ml) whole milk
5 egg yolks
2 tablespoons light corn syrup
½ teaspoon vanilla extract (essence)

Caramelized sugar is the secret to this silky treat. Be sure to allow the syrup to turn a deep caramel color for the best flavor.

In a medium-sized, heavy saucepan over medium-low heat, combine the sugar and water. Stir until the sugar dissolves, about 5 minutes. Using a pastry brush dipped in water, brush down any sugar crystals that form on the pan sides. Increase the heat to high and boil without stirring until the syrup is a deep caramel color, gently swirling the pan occasionally for even caramelization, about 10 minutes (timing depends upon the size and weight of the pan and the intensity of the heat).

Gradually add the milk to the caramel; the mixture will bubble vigorously. Reduce the heat to medium-low and stir until all the hard bits of caramel melt, about 5 minutes.

In a metal bowl, whisk together the egg yolks and corn syrup until blended. Form a kitchen towel into a ring and place the bowl on top to prevent it from moving. Gradually pour the hot caramel into the yolk mixture, whisking constantly. Return the mixture to the same saucepan and place over medium-low heat. Cook, stirring slowly and continuously with a wooden spatula, until the custard thickens and leaves a path on the back of the spatula when a finger is drawn across it, about 6 minutes; do not allow to boil. Pour the custard through a medium-mesh sieve set over a clean bowl. Refrigerate until cold, about 1 hour.

Stir in the vanilla. Transfer the custard to an ice cream maker and process according to the manufacturer's instructions. For the best texture, serve the gelato immediately. Or transfer to a container, cover and freeze until firm, at least 4 hours or for up to 3 days. (Note: the longer freezing results in a texture more like that of ice cream.)

Makes about 2¾ cups (22 fl oz/680 ml); serves 3 or 4

Banana Gelato

2 cups (16 fl oz/500 ml) whole milk
5 egg yolks
¾ cup (6 oz/185 g) sugar
2 tablespoons light corn syrup
½ cup (2 oz/60 g) walnuts, optional
1½ cups (9 oz/280 g) sliced very ripe banana (about 2 large bananas)
1 tablespoon fresh lemon juice

The rich banana flavor and dense creaminess of this gelato make it a surefire favorite. Add the sprinkling of walnuts, if you like, or leave it plain to savor its perfectly smooth texture.

Pour the milk into a medium-sized, heavy saucepan. Bring to a simmer over medium-high heat. Remove from the heat.

In a metal bowl, whisk together the egg yolks, sugar and corn syrup until blended. Form a kitchen towel into a ring and place the bowl on top to prevent it from moving. Gradually pour the hot milk into the yolk mixture, whisking constantly. Return the mixture to the same saucepan and place over medium-low heat. Cook, stirring slowly and continuously with a wooden spatula, until the custard thickens and leaves a path on the back of the spatula when a finger is drawn across it, about 6 minutes; do not allow to boil.

Pour the custard through a medium-mesh sieve set over a clean bowl. Refrigerate until cold, about 1 hour.

Meanwhile, if using the walnuts, preheat an oven to 350°F (180°C). Spread the walnuts on a baking sheet and bake until lightly toasted and fragrant, about 10 minutes. Remove from the oven, let cool, then chop finely. Set aside.

In a food processor fitted with the metal blade or in a blender, combine the bananas and lemon juice and purée until smooth. Stir into the chilled custard.

Transfer the custard to an ice cream maker and process according to the manufacturer's instructions. Add the walnuts, if using, during the final minute of processing. For the best texture, serve the gelato immediately. Or transfer to a container, cover and freeze until firm, at least 4 hours or for up to 3 days. (Note: the longer freezing results in a texture more like that of ice cream.)

Makes about 3½ cups (28 fl oz/875 ml); serves 4–6

Double Espresso Gelato

2 cups (16 fl oz/500 ml) whole milk
½ cup (2 oz/60 g) espresso-roast coffee beans
5 egg yolks
¾ cup (6 oz/185 g) sugar
2 tablespoons light corn syrup
1 teaspoon instant espresso powder
½ teaspoon vanilla extract (essence)

A double dose of espresso from coffee beans and espresso powder gives this gelato its deep, rich flavor.

In a medium-sized, heavy saucepan, combine the milk and coffee beans. Bring to a simmer over medium-high heat. Remove from the heat. Cover and let stand for 30 minutes.

Pour the milk through a medium-mesh sieve set over a bowl; set aside. In a metal bowl, whisk together the egg yolks, sugar and corn syrup until blended. Form a kitchen towel into a ring and place the metal bowl on top to prevent it from moving. Gradually pour the milk into the yolk mixture, whisking constantly. Return the mixture to the same saucepan and place over medium-low heat. Cook, stirring slowly and continuously with a wooden spatula, until the custard thickens and leaves a path on the back of the spatula when a finger is drawn across it, about 6 minutes; do not allow to boil.

Pour the custard through the medium-mesh sieve set over a clean bowl. Add the espresso powder and vanilla and stir until the espresso dissolves. Refrigerate until cold, about 1 hour.

Transfer the custard to an ice cream maker and process according to the manufacturer's instructions. For the best texture, serve the gelato immediately. Or transfer to a container, cover and freeze until firm, at least 4 hours or for up to 3 days. (Note: the longer freezing results in a texture more like that of ice cream.)

Makes about 2½ cups (20 fl oz/625 ml); serves 3 or 4

Crimson Plum-Raspberry Sorbet

1 cup (8 oz/250 g) sugar
⅔ cup (5 fl oz/160 ml) water
2 tablespoons light corn syrup
1 package (1 lb/500 g) frozen unsweetened raspberries, thawed
1 lb (500 g) ripe plums, preferably red-fleshed, halved, pitted and sliced

The bright color of this sorbet is a good indication of its equally intense fresh fruit flavor. Garnish with fresh raspberries and fresh mint leaves, if you like.

In a small, heavy saucepan over low heat, combine the sugar, water and corn syrup. Stir until the sugar dissolves, about 3 minutes. Increase the heat to high and bring to a boil. Remove from the heat and set the syrup aside.

In a food processor fitted with the metal blade or in a blender, place the raspberries and their juices. Purée until smooth. Strain the purée through a coarse sieve set over a bowl to remove the seeds. Press firmly on the solids with a rubber spatula to extract as much liquid as possible; discard the solids.

Return the berry purée to the processor or blender. Add the plums and purée until smooth. Add the reserved syrup and process to mix well. Transfer to a bowl and refrigerate until cold, about 1 hour.

Transfer the sorbet mixture to an ice cream maker and process according to the manufacturer's instructions. Transfer the sorbet to a container; cover and freeze until firm, at least 4 hours or for up to 3 days.

Makes about 5 cups (40 fl oz/1.25 l); serves 8

Lemon-Lime Granita

2 cups (16 fl oz/500 ml) water
1 cup (8 oz/250 g) sugar
⅓ cup (3 fl oz/80 ml) fresh lemon juice
⅓ cup (3 fl oz/80 ml) fresh lime juice
4 lime slices, each ⅛ inch (3 mm) thick and a slit cut into each

Offer this refreshing treat after a hearty Mexican or southwestern meal. For a festive presentation, serve in chilled margarita glasses.

In a medium-sized, heavy saucepan, combine the water and sugar. Place over medium heat and stir until the sugar dissolves, about 3 minutes. Increase the heat to high and bring to a boil. Remove from the heat and let cool.

Stir in the lemon and lime juices and pour the mixture into a metal bowl. Freeze, whisking every 30 minutes, until semifirm, about 3 hours. Cover and freeze without stirring until frozen solid, at least 8 hours or as long as 24 hours.

At least 1 hour before serving, place 4 margarita glasses or wine glasses in the freezer.

To serve, using a fork, scrape the surface of the granita to form ice crystals. Scoop the crystals into the frozen glasses. Place a lime slice on the rim of each glass and serve immediately.

Serves 4

Rich Chocolate-Orange Sorbet

¾ cup (6 oz/185 g) sugar
¾ cup (2½ oz/75 g) unsweetened cocoa
1½ cups (12 fl oz/375 ml) water
2 oz (60 g) European bittersweet chocolate, chopped
⅔ cup (5 fl oz/160 ml) fresh orange juice
2 tablespoons light corn syrup
1 tablespoon grated orange zest

For those watching their fat intake, this soft, creamy sorbet is especially welcome. Despite its healthful character, it is just as satisfying as ice cream.

In a medium-sized, heavy saucepan, combine the sugar and cocoa. Gradually whisk in the water. Place over medium-high heat and bring to a boil, whisking constantly, about 4 minutes. Reduce the heat to low. Add the chocolate, orange juice, corn syrup and orange zest and stir just until the chocolate melts. Pour into a bowl and refrigerate until cold, about 1 hour.

Transfer the sorbet mixture to an ice cream maker and process according to the manufacturer's instructions. Transfer the sorbet to a container; cover and freeze overnight to allow the flavors to develop, or for up to 3 days.

Makes about 2¼ cups (18 fl oz/560 ml); serves 3 or 4

Dried Apricot Sorbet

1¼ cups (10 fl oz/310 ml) water
1 can (11½ fl oz/355 ml) apricot nectar
¾ cup (4½ oz/140 g) dried apricots
¾ cup (6 oz/185 g) sugar
2 tablespoons light corn syrup
2 tablespoons fresh lemon juice

Dried apricots and apricot nectar give this sorbet its bright orange color and intense flavor.

In a large, heavy saucepan, combine the water, nectar and apricots. Place over medium-low heat, cover and cook, stirring occasionally, until the apricots are very tender, about 25 minutes. Add the sugar, corn syrup and lemon juice, stirring until the sugar dissolves, about 3 minutes. Remove from the heat.

In a food processor fitted with the metal blade or in a blender, purée the apricot mixture until smooth. Pour the purée into a bowl. Refrigerate until cold, about 2 hours.

Transfer the sorbet mixture to an ice cream maker and process according to the manufacturer's instructions. Transfer the sorbet to a container; cover and freeze until firm, at least 4 hours or for up to 3 days.

Makes about 3¾ cups (30 fl oz/940 ml); serves 4–6

Raspberry Granita

2 cups (8 oz/250 g) fresh raspberries or frozen unsweetened raspberries, thawed
1¼ cups (10 fl oz/310 ml) water
½ cup (4 oz/125 g) plus 2 tablespoons sugar

Pretty and refreshing, this fruity granita is terrific after any meal or as a cooling afternoon treat on a hot day.

In a food processor fitted with the metal blade or in a blender, combine the raspberries, water and sugar. Purée until smooth. Pour the purée through a coarse sieve set over a metal bowl to remove the seeds. Press firmly on the solids with a rubber spatula to extract as much liquid as possible; discard the solids.

Freeze the purée, whisking every 30 minutes, until semi-firm, about 3 hours. Cover and freeze without stirring until frozen solid, at least 8 hours or as long as 24 hours.

At least 1 hour before serving, place 4 martini glasses or wine glasses in the freezer.

To serve, using a fork, scrape the surface of the granita to form ice crystals. Scoop the crystals into the frozen glasses and serve immediately.

Serves 4

Tangerine Sorbet

3 cups (24 fl oz/750 ml) fresh tangerine juice (from about 4 lb/2 kg tangerines)
1 cup (8 oz/250 g) sugar
2 tablespoons light corn syrup
1 teaspoon grated tangerine zest

This sweet-tart sorbet is the perfect finale to a rich winter meal. It can also be made with oranges.

In a medium-sized, heavy saucepan, combine 1 cup (8 fl oz/250 ml) of the tangerine juice, the sugar, corn syrup and tangerine zest. Place over medium heat and stir until the sugar dissolves, about 3 minutes. Pour into a bowl. Stir in the remaining 2 cups (16 fl oz/500 ml) juice. Refrigerate until cold, about 1 hour.

Transfer the sorbet mixture to an ice cream maker and process according to the manufacturer's instructions. Transfer the sorbet to a container; cover and freeze until firm, at least 4 hours or for up to 3 days.

Makes about 4 cups (32 fl oz/1 l); serves 6

Pineapple-Yogurt Sherbet

1 tablespoon water
½ teaspoon unflavored gelatin
1 can (8 oz/250 g) crushed unsweetened pineapple
⅔ cup (5 oz/155 g) sugar
¼ cup (2 fl oz/60 ml) light corn syrup
1 cup (8 oz/250 g) plain nonfat yogurt

This fat-free treat is simple to make and has a light, refreshing flavor.

Pour the water into a small cup. Sprinkle the gelatin over the water and let stand for 10 minutes to soften.

In a medium-sized, heavy saucepan, combine the pineapple, sugar and corn syrup. Place over medium heat and stir until the sugar dissolves, about 2 minutes. Increase the heat to high and bring to a boil. Remove from the heat.

Add the gelatin mixture to the pineapple mixture and stir until the gelatin dissolves, about 1 minute. In a food processor fitted with the metal blade or in a blender, purée the pineapple mixture until smooth. Add the yogurt and process to mix well. Refrigerate until cold, about 1 hour.

Transfer the sherbet mixture to an ice cream maker and process according to the manufacturer's instructions. Transfer the sherbet to a container; cover and freeze until firm, at least 4 hours or for up to 3 days.

Makes about 3 cups (24 fl oz/750 ml); serves 4

Red Burgundy–Cinnamon Granita

2 cups (16 fl oz/500 ml) red Burgundy wine
1 cup (8 fl oz/250 ml) water
¾ cup (6 oz/185 g) sugar
1 cinnamon stick, 3 inches (7.5 cm) long

Burgundy wine gives this icy treat a deep crimson color. For an elegant touch, serve it in martini glasses and garnish with cinnamon sticks.

In a medium-sized, heavy saucepan, combine the wine, water, sugar and cinnamon stick. Place over medium heat and stir until the sugar dissolves, about 3 minutes. Increase the heat to high and bring to a boil. Remove from the heat. Cover and let stand for 1 hour.

Remove the cinnamon stick and discard. Pour the mixture into a metal bowl. Freeze, whisking every 30 minutes, until semifirm, about 3 hours. Cover and freeze without stirring until frozen solid, at least 8 hours or as long as 24 hours.

At least 1 hour before serving, place 4 martini glasses or wine glasses in the freezer.

To serve, using a fork, scrape the surface of the granita to form ice crystals. Scoop the crystals into the frozen glasses and serve immediately.

Serves 4

Fall Pear-Cardamom Sorbet

- 4 cardamom pods, lightly crushed
- 2¼ lb (1.1 kg) ripe pears such as Bartlett (Williams') or Comice, peeled, quartered and cored
- 1¾ cups (14 fl oz/430 ml) Gewürztraminer wine
- ¾ cup (6 oz/185 g) sugar
- 2 tablespoons light corn syrup

Cardamom pods, available in the spice section of most food stores, add an exotic flavor to this creamy sorbet. Be sure to use the ripest fruit available.

Wrap the cardamom pods in a small piece of triple-thick cheesecloth (muslin) and tie in a tight bundle. In a medium-sized, heavy saucepan, combine the cardamom bundle, pears and 1 cup (8 fl oz/250 ml) of the wine. Place over medium heat, cover and cook, stirring occasionally, until the pears are tender, about 10 minutes. Remove the cardamom bundle and discard. Add the sugar and corn syrup and stir over medium heat until the sugar dissolves, about 3 minutes. Remove from the heat.

In a food processor fitted with the metal blade or in a blender, purée the pear mixture. Pour the purée into a bowl. Stir in the remaining ¾ cup (6 fl oz/180 ml) wine. Refrigerate until cold, about 1 hour.

Transfer the sorbet mixture to an ice cream maker and process according to the manufacturer's instructions. Transfer the sorbet to a container; cover and freeze until firm, at least 4 hours or for up to 3 days.

Makes about 4½ cups (36 fl oz/1.1 l); serves 6–8

Espresso-Orange Granita

1 large orange
2 cups (16 fl oz/500 ml) water
½ cup (4 oz/125 g) plus 2 tablespoons sugar
4 teaspoons instant espresso powder
½ cup (4 fl oz/125 ml) heavy (double) cream, chilled
¼ teaspoon grated orange zest

In Italy, this particular granita is traditionally topped with sweetened whipped cream. The granita will melt quickly, so be sure the wine glasses have been chilled in the freezer for at least 1 hour before filling them.

Using a vegetable peeler, remove the zest from the orange in wide strips. Place the strips in a medium-sized, heavy saucepan and add the water, the ½ cup (4 oz/125 g) sugar and the espresso powder. Place over medium heat and stir until the sugar dissolves and the mixture is hot, about 3 minutes. Remove from the heat. Cover and let stand for 10 minutes.

Pour the mixture through a coarse sieve set over a metal bowl. Freeze, whisking every 30 minutes, until semifirm, about 3 hours. Cover and freeze without stirring until frozen solid, at least 8 hours or as long as 24 hours.

At least 1 hour before serving, place 4 wine glasses in the freezer.

In a bowl, combine the cream, the 2 tablespoons sugar and the orange zest. Using an electric mixer set on medium-high speed, beat until soft peaks form. Cover and refrigerate until ready to use, or for up to 1 hour.

To serve, using a fork, scrape the surface of the granita to form ice crystals. Scoop the crystals into the frozen wine glasses. Top with the whipped cream and serve at once.

Serves 4

Mango Sorbet

2 large ripe mangoes
6 tablespoons (3 oz/90 g) sugar
¼ cup (2 fl oz/60 ml) light corn syrup

Mangoes have naturally bright yellow flesh that is magnificent in a sorbet. This is the ideal finish to a spicy Asian meal.

Using a small, sharp knife, make 4 lengthwise slits through the skin of the mango, cutting the skin into quarters. Peel off the skin and discard. Then slice the flesh from both sides of the large flat pit, as well as from around its edges.

Place the mango flesh in a food processor fitted with the metal blade or in a blender; purée until smooth. Measure the purée; you should have 1⅔ cups (13 fl oz/410 ml). Return the purée to the processor or blender. Add the sugar and corn syrup and process to mix well. Pour the purée into a bowl and refrigerate until cold, about 1 hour.

Transfer the sorbet mixture to an ice cream maker and process according to the manufacturer's instructions. Transfer the sorbet to a container; cover and freeze until firm, at least 4 hours or for up to 3 days.

Makes about 2½ cups (20 fl oz/625 ml); serves 3 or 4

Cantaloupe Sorbet with Minted Melon

The sorbet looks beautiful served in a cantaloupe half and topped with a variety of diced melons. To make a particularly pretty presentation, use a small, sharp knife to cut a zigzag edge on each melon half and garnish each serving with a mint sprig. Essencia, a sweet dessert wine made from orange muscat grapes, imparts a delicate flavor and texture. If you can't find Essencia, substitute a late-harvest Riesling or Sauterne.

FOR THE SORBET:

2 lb (1 kg) cantaloupe, halved, seeded, peeled and cut into large pieces
½ cup (4 fl oz/125 ml) Essencia or other sweet dessert wine *(see note)*
½ cup (4 oz/125 g) sugar
2 tablespoons light corn syrup

FOR THE MINTED MELON:

1 tablespoon sugar
1 tablespoon sliced fresh mint leaves
1 cup (6 oz/185 g) peeled, seeded and diced cantaloupe (¼-inch/6-mm dice)
1 cup (6 oz/185 g) peeled, seeded and diced honeydew melon (¼-inch/6-mm dice)
1 cup (6 oz/185 g) peeled, seeded and diced watermelon (¼-inch/6-mm dice)
2 small cantaloupes, halved, seeded and partially hollowed out, optional

To make the sorbet, in a food processor fitted with the metal blade or in a blender, purée the cantaloupe until smooth. You should have about 2⅓ cups (19 fl oz/580 ml) purée. Transfer to a bowl and add the dessert wine, sugar and corn syrup. Stir until the sugar dissolves, about 2 minutes. Transfer to an ice cream maker and process according to the manufacturer's instructions. Transfer the sorbet to a container; cover and freeze until firm, at least 4 hours or for up to 3 days.

To prepare the minted melon, in a large bowl, combine the sugar and mint and mash lightly with the back of a spoon. Add the diced cantaloupe, honeydew and watermelon and toss to coat. Let stand for 5 minutes.

To serve, scoop the sorbet into the melon halves, if using, or into chilled bowls. Spoon the diced fruit evenly over each serving.

Makes about 3½ cups (28 fl oz/875 ml) sorbet; serves 4

Strawberry-Rhubarb Sherbet

- 2 tablespoons water
- 1 teaspoon unflavored gelatin
- 1 package (1 lb/500 g) frozen unsweetened sliced rhubarb, thawed
- 1 package (1 lb/500 g) frozen unsweetened whole strawberries, thawed
- 1½ cups (12 oz/375 g) sugar
- 1½ cups (12 fl oz/375 ml) whole milk
- ½ cup (4 fl oz/125 ml) light corn syrup

Inspired by a favorite pie, the combination of strawberries and rhubarb also makes a great sherbet. The rhubarb lends a distinctive tangy flavor.

Pour the water into a small cup. Sprinkle the gelatin over the water. Let stand for 10 minutes to soften.

Meanwhile, in a large, heavy saucepan, combine the thawed rhubarb and strawberries with their juices and the sugar. Place over medium heat and stir until the sugar dissolves, about 3 minutes. Continue cooking, stirring occasionally, until the rhubarb is tender, about 5 minutes.

Add the gelatin mixture to the hot rhubarb mixture and stir until the gelatin dissolves, about 1 minute.

In a food processor fitted with the metal blade or in a blender, purée the rhubarb mixture until smooth. Pour the purée into a large bowl. Add the milk and corn syrup and stir to blend. Refrigerate until cold, about 1 hour.

Transfer the sherbet mixture to an ice cream maker and process according to the manufacturer's instructions. Transfer the sherbet to a container; cover and freeze until firm, at least 4 hours or for up to 3 days.

Makes about 5 cups (40 fl oz/1.25 l); serves 8

Apple Cider Granita

2 cups (16 fl oz/500 ml) apple cider
1/3 cup (3 oz/90 g) firmly packed light brown sugar
10 whole cloves
10 allspice berries

Offer this granita after a hearty autumn dinner that features roast pork or duck and a potato gratin.

In a medium-sized, heavy saucepan, combine the apple cider, brown sugar, cloves and allspice. Place over medium-high heat and stir until the sugar dissolves and the mixture is hot, about 3 minutes. Remove from the heat. Cover and let stand for 1 hour.

Pour the cider mixture through a coarse sieve set over a metal bowl. Freeze, whisking every 30 minutes, until semifirm, about 3 hours. Cover and freeze without stirring until frozen solid, at least 8 hours or as long as overnight.

At least 1 hour before serving, place 4 glass bowls or wine glasses in the freezer.

To serve, using a fork, scrape the surface of the granita to form ice crystals. Scoop the crystals into the frozen glasses and serve immediately.

Serves 4

Tropical Litchi Sorbet

3 cans (11 oz/345 g each) peeled whole litchis in heavy syrup
6 tablespoons (3 fl oz/90 ml) water
3 tablespoons sugar
1 tablespoon peeled and grated fresh ginger
3 tablespoons light corn syrup

Offer this refreshing treat after a spicy Chinese or Thai dinner and pass some almond cookies. You will find litchis in the international or Asian food section of well-stocked food stores or in Asian markets.

Drain the litchis, reserving ¾ cup (6 fl oz/180 ml) of the syrup. Place the litchis and the reserved syrup in a food processor fitted with the metal blade or in a blender. Set aside.

In a small, heavy saucepan over medium heat, combine the water, sugar and ginger. Stir until the sugar dissolves, about 2 minutes. Increase the heat to high and bring to a boil. Remove from the heat and add to the litchis in the processor or blender. Purée until smooth. Pour the purée through a coarse sieve set over a bowl, pressing on the solids with a rubber spatula to extract as much of the liquid as possible; discard the solids. Stir in the corn syrup. Refrigerate until cold, about 1 hour.

Transfer the sorbet mixture to an ice cream maker and process according to the manufacturer's instructions. Transfer the sorbet to a container; cover and freeze until firm, at least 4 hours or for up to 3 days.

Makes about 3 cups (24 fl oz/750 ml); serves 4

Glossary

The following glossary defines terms specifically as they relate to ice creams and frozen desserts, including major and unusual ingredients and basic techniques.

Allspice
Sweet spice of Caribbean origin with a flavor suggesting a blend of **cinnamon, cloves** and **nutmeg,** hence its name. May be purchased as whole dried berries or ground. When using whole berries, they may be bruised—gently crushed with the bottom of a pan or other heavy instrument—to release more of their flavor.

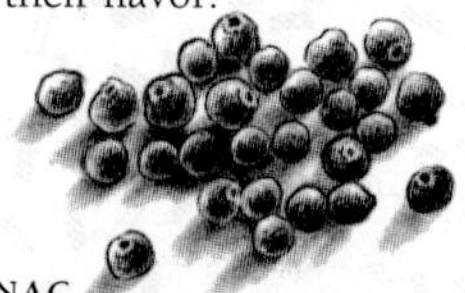

Armagnac
Dry brandy, similar to **Cognac,** distilled in—and made from wine produced in—the Armagnac region of southwestern France. If unavailable, other good-quality dry wine-based brandies may be substituted.

Baking Soda
Also known as sodium bicarbonate or bicarbonate of soda, the active component of baking powder and the source of carbon dioxide gas often used as a leavener in batters that include acidic ingredients. In brittles and other caramelized candies, baking soda foams when it reacts chemically to the acid in caramelized sugar, producing a candy that is porous and tender.

Berries
A wide variety of cultivated berries adds bright color, flavor and texture to frozen desserts. Usually sold in small containers or baskets, they should be checked carefully to make sure that they are firm, plump, and free of blemishes, bruises or mold. Frozen berries, available in the freezer section of food stores, may be substituted and are actually preferred in some frozen desserts. Berry varieties used in this book include:

Blackberries. Juicy, lustrous purple-black berries, at peak of season in summer.
Blueberries. Small, round berries with smooth, dark blue skins, available from late spring through summer.
Boysenberries. A cross of the blackberry, raspberry and loganberry, and blending their distinctive flavors and colors, this variety (below) is noted for its large, plump size and juicy sweetness.

Strawberries. Probably the most popular berry variety, these plump and juicy, intensely sweet, red, heart-shaped fruits are at their peak from spring into midsummer.

Butter, Unsalted
For dessert making, unsalted butter is preferred.

Chocolate
When making frozen desserts, purchase the best-quality chocolate you can find. Many cooks prefer the quality of European chocolate made in Switzerland, Belgium, France or Italy.

Bittersweet Chocolate
Lightly sweetened eating or baking chocolate. Look for bittersweet chocolate that contains at least 50 percent cocoa butter.

White Chocolate
A chocolatelike product for eating or baking, made by combining pure cocoa butter with sugar, powdered milk and sometimes vanilla. Check labels to make sure that the white chocolate you buy is made exclusively with cocoa butter, without the addition of coconut oil or vegetable shortening.

To Chop Chocolate
First, break the chocolate by hand into small chunks, handling it as little as possible to avoid melting. Then, using a heavy knife and a clean, dry, odor-free chopping surface, carefully chop the chocolate into smaller pieces.

Steadying the knife tip with your hand, continue chopping across the pieces until the desired consistency is reached.

Cardamom
Sweet, exotic-tasting spice mainly used in East Indian cooking and in Middle Eastern and Eastern European cuisines. Its small, round seeds, which grow enclosed inside a husklike pod, may be purchased whole or already ground. Grind whole seeds with a spice grinder or crush with a mortar and pestle as needed.

Cinnamon
Popular sweet spice for flavoring desserts. The aromatic bark of a type of evergreen tree, it is sold ground or as whole dried strips known as cinnamon sticks (below).

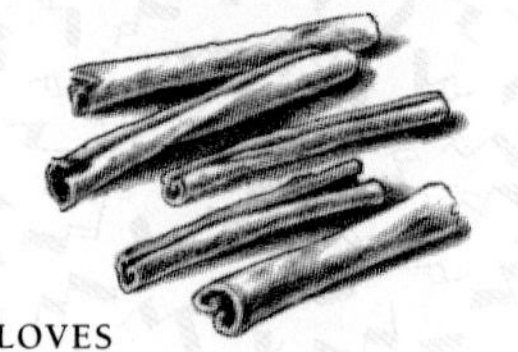

Cloves
Rich and aromatic East African spice. Used whole to add flavor to frozen desserts. Also used ground as a popular spice in both sweet and savory dishes.

Cocoa, Unsweetened
Richly flavored, fine-textured powder ground from the solids left after much of the cocoa butter has been extracted from chocolate liquor. Cocoa specially treated to reduce its natural acidity, resulting in a darker color and more mellow flavor, is known as Dutch-process cocoa.

Coconut
For baking purposes, shredded or flaked coconut is sold ready-to-use in cans or plastic packages in the baking section of most food stores. The label of each package will indicate whether the product is sweetened or unsweetened; most frozen dessert recipes call for sweetened coconut. Be sure to purchase the coconut from a store with a rapid turnover, to ensure freshness.

Canned sweetened cream of coconut, a rich and thick concentrate of the fruit's liquid and fat, is available in the baking or liquor section.

Cognac
Dry spirit distilled from wine and, strictly speaking, produced in the Cognac region of France. Other good-quality dry wine-based brandies may be substituted.

Corn Syrup
Neutral-tasting syrup extracted from corn. Sold either as light corn syrup or dark corn syrup, which has added color and flavor.

Cream, Sour
Commercial dairy product, made from pasteurized sweet cream, with a tangy flavor and thick, smooth consistency.

Cream, Heavy
Cream with a butterfat content of at least 36 percent. For the best flavor and cooking properties, purchase fresh cream, avoiding long-lasting varieties that have been processed by ultraheat methods. In Britain, use double cream.

Crème de Cassis
Sweet, red liqueur made by steeping black currants in grape brandy.

Espresso
The strong taste of espresso-roast coffee beans provides distinctive flavor to frozen desserts. For an easily blended source of this intense flavor, use instant espresso powder or granules, found in the coffee section of food stores, Italian delicatessens or specialty coffee stores.

Extracts
Flavorings derived by dissolving essential oils of richly flavored foods, such as almonds, peppermint and vanilla, in an alcohol base. Use only products labeled "pure" or "natural" extract (essence).

Gelatin, Unflavored
Unflavored commercial gelatin gives delicate body to some frozen desserts. Sold in envelopes holding about 1 tablespoon (¼ oz/7 g), each of which is sufficient to jell about 2 cups (16 fl oz/500 ml) liquid.

Gewürztraminer
Semidry white wine from Alsace, noted for its assertive and spicy flavor and fragrant bouquet.

Ginger
The rhizome of the tropical ginger plant (below), which yields a sweet, strong-flavored spice. Ground dried ginger is available in the spice section of food stores.

Candied or crystallized ginger is made by first preserving pieces of ginger in sugar syrup and then coating them with granulated sugar; it is available in specialty-food shops or in the baking or Asian food sections of well-stocked stores.

Grand Marnier
A popular commercial brand of orange-flavored liqueur, distinguished by its pure **Cognac** base.

Half-and-half
A commercial dairy product consisting of half milk and half light cream. Known as half cream in Britain.

Honey
The natural, sweet, syruplike substance produced by bees from flower nectar, honey subtly reflects the color, taste and aroma of the blossoms from which it was made. Milder varieties, such as clover and orange blossom, are lighter in color and better suited to general cooking purposes. Provides a distinctive mellow sweetness in some frozen desserts.

Kahlúa
Commercial Mexican brand of coffee liqueur. Other brands may be substituted.

Litchis
Also frequently spelled lychees, these walnut-sized Chinese fruits are noted for their pearl-colored, sweet flesh, somewhat reminiscent of grapes in taste and texture, concealed in a brittle reddish brown skin. Although available fresh in well-stocked food stores and Asian markets from late spring to midsummer, they are more frequently purchased canned, either in water or heavy sugar syrup.

Eggs
Although eggs are sold in the United States in a range of standard sizes, large grade A eggs are the most common size and should be used for the recipes in this book.

To separate an egg, crack the shell in half by tapping it against the side of a bowl and then breaking it apart with your fingers. Holding the shell halves over the bowl, gently transfer the whole yolk back and forth between them, letting the clear white drop away into the bowl. Take care not to break the yolk. Transfer the yolk to another bowl.

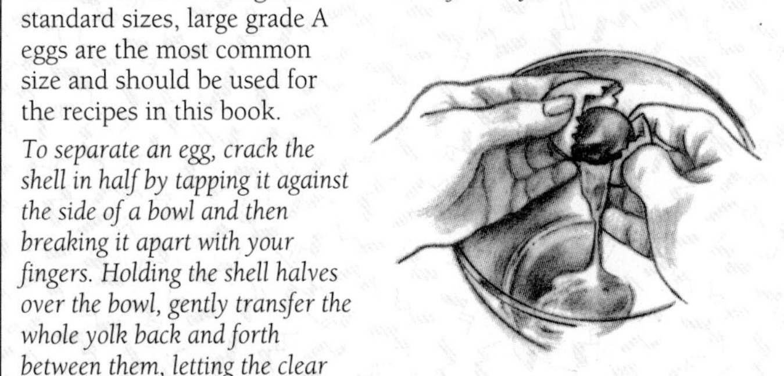

Alternatively, gently pour the egg from the shell onto the slightly cupped fingers of your clean, outstretched hand, held over a bowl. Let the whites fall between your fingers into the bowl; the whole yolk will remain in your hand.

The same basic function is also performed by an aluminum, ceramic or plastic egg separator placed over a bowl. The separator holds the yolk intact in its cuplike center while allowing the white to drip out through one or more slots in its side into the bowl.

Nuts
Rich and mellow in flavor, crisp and crunchy in texture, a wide variety of nuts complements frozen desserts. For the best selection, look in a specialty-food shop, health-food store or the food market baking section. Some of the most popular options include:

Almonds
Mellow, sweet-flavored nuts (below) that are an important crop in California and are popular throughout the world.

Hazelnuts
Small, usually spherical nuts (below) with a slightly sweet flavor. Grown in Italy, Spain and the United States. Also known as filberts.

Macadamias
Spherical nuts (below), about twice the diameter of hazelnuts, with a very rich, buttery flavor and crisp texture. Native to Australia, they are now grown primarily in Hawaii.

Peanuts
Not true nuts, these are actually legumes produced on a low-branching plant. When roasted, they have a rich, full flavor and satisfying crispness that make them the world's most popular nut. The Virginia variety is longer and more oval than the smaller, rounder, red-skinned Spanish peanut. Native to South America, peanuts are an important crop in Africa and the United States.

Pecans
Brown-skinned, crinkly textured nuts (below) with a distinctive sweet, rich flavor and crisp, slightly crumbly texture. Native to the southern United States.

Pine Nuts
Small, ivory seeds (below) extracted from the cones of a species of pine tree, with a rich, slightly resinous flavor.

Pistachios
Slightly sweet, full-flavored nuts (below) with green, crunchy meat. Native to Asia Minor, they are grown primarily in the Middle East and California.

Walnuts
Rich, crisp-textured nuts with distinctively crinkled surfaces. English walnuts, the most familiar variety (below), are grown worldwide, although the largest crops are in California.

To Toast Nuts
Toasting brings out the full flavor and aroma of nuts. To toast nuts, preheat an oven to 350°F (180°C). Spread the nuts in a single layer on a baking sheet and toast until they just begin to change color, 5–10 minutes or 3 minutes for pine nuts. Remove from the oven and let cool.

Toasting also loosens the skins of nuts such as hazelnuts and walnuts, which may be removed by wrapping the still-warm nuts in a kitchen towel and rubbing against them with the palms of your hands.

To Chop Nuts
To chop nuts, spread them in a single layer on a nonslip cutting surface. Using a chef's knife, carefully chop the nuts with a gentle rocking motion. Alternatively, put a handful or two of nuts in a food processor fitted with the metal blade and use a few rapid on-off pulses to chop the nuts to desired consistency; repeat with the remaining nuts in batches. Be careful not to process the nuts too long or their oils will be released and the nuts will turn into a paste.

Mangoes
Tropical fruits with a very juicy, aromatic orange flesh. Ripe mangoes yield slightly to finger pressure; ripen firm mangoes at room temperature in an open paper bag or plastic bag.

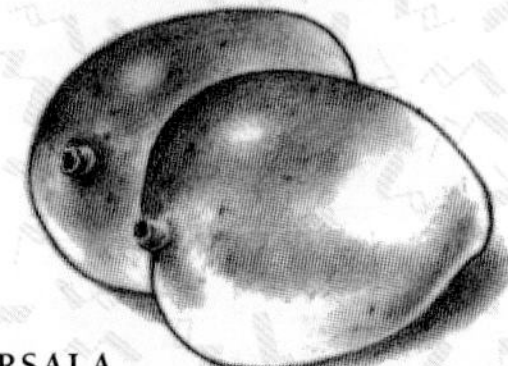

Marsala
Dry or sweet amber Italian fortified wine from the region around Marsala, in Sicily.

Milk, Whole
Whole milk (regular vitamin D homogenized milk) is preferred for the recipes in this book. It contains a minimum of 3.5 percent fat and imparts a smooth texture and rich flavor.

Mint
Refreshing sweet herb used fresh to flavor some frozen desserts.

Nutmeg
Popular sweet spice that is the hard pit of the fruit of the nutmeg tree. May be bought already ground or, for fresher flavor, whole. Whole nutmegs may be kept inside special nutmeg graters, which include hinged flaps that conceal a storage compartment.

Peaches
Juicy, sweet and fragrant, the peach ranks as one of the most glorious of summertime's fruit. Although most peaches sold in markets today have had some of the characteristic fuzz mechanically removed from their skins, enabling them to be simply rinsed and eaten, they nevertheless require peeling before use in frozen desserts.

Peeling Peaches
Bring a large saucepan three-fourths full of water to a boil and fill a large bowl with ice and water. One at a time, immerse each peach in the water to loosen its skin, about 10 seconds; then transfer it to the bowl of ice water to cool it briefly. Use your fingers or a small, sharp knife to peel away the skin.

Pitting Peaches
Using a small, sharp knife, cut the peach in half down to the pit, cutting through the stem end and following the slight indention or ridge along one side of the peach. Grasp the two halves of the cut peach with your hands and twist, pulling them apart.

Pull out the pit from the half within which it remains. If it clings to the peach, use a knife to carefully pry or cut it out.

Pears
The subtle sweetness and texture of pears work surprisingly well in some frozen desserts. Bartlett pears (below, right), also called Williams' pears, are medium-sized and shaped roughly like bells, with creamy yellow skins sometimes tinged with red; fine-textured, juicy and mild tasting, they are equally good for cooking or eating and are available from summer to early autumn. Comice pears (below, left), available from autumn through early winter, are sweet and juicy; large, round and short-necked, they have greenish yellow skins tinged with red.

Pumpkin, Canned Solid-Pack
The seedless orange purée of pumpkin meat is available canned in most food stores.

Rhubarb
Perennial plant whose stems resemble large, salmon-colored celery stalks. Although a vegetable, rhubarb is most commonly eaten as a fruit, cooked and sweetened with sugar and often combined with strawberries or raspberries. Avoid the leaves and roots, which can be toxic. Frozen rhubarb pieces are available in the freezer section of well-stocked food stores.

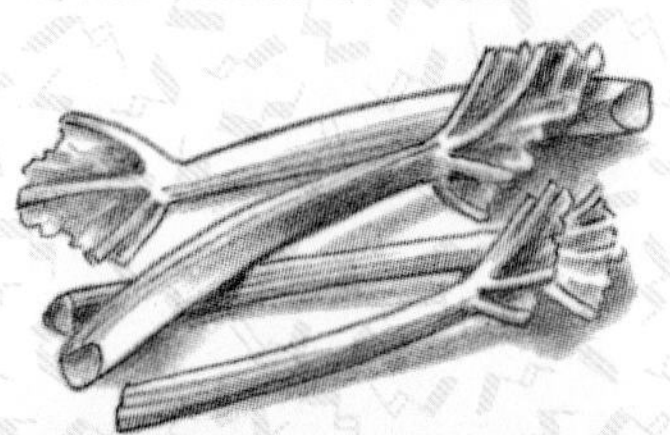

Riesling, Late-Harvest
Variety of sweet dessert wine made from spicy Riesling grapes that have been left on the vine until they shrivel and intensify in sweetness.

Scotch Whisky
A mellow, dry, golden brown spirit originating in Scotland, distilled from malted barley and matured in oak casks for at least three years.

Sugar
Many different forms of sugar may be used to sweeten frozen desserts.

Brown Sugar. A rich-tasting granulated sugar combined with molasses in varying quantities to yield golden, light or dark brown sugar, with crystals varying from coarse to fine. Widely available in the baking section of food stores.

Confectioners' Sugar. Finely pulverized sugar, also known as powdered or icing sugar, which dissolves quickly and provides a thin, white decorative coating. To prevent confectioners' sugar from absorbing moisture in the air and caking, manufacturers often mix a little cornstarch into it.

Granulated Sugar. The standard, widely used form of pure white sugar. Do not use superfine granulated sugar (also known as castor sugar) unless specified.

Vanilla
One of the most popular flavorings in dessert making, vanilla beans are the dried aromatic pods of a variety of orchid. Although vanilla is most commonly used in the form of an alcohol-based extract (essence), the whole bean and particularly the seeds inside it are a good source of pure vanilla flavor. Vanilla extract or beans from Madagascar are the best. For directions on seeding vanilla beans, see page 9.

Yogurt, Plain Nonfat
Milk fermented by bacterial cultures that impart a mildly acidic flavor and custardlike texture. So-called plain yogurt simply refers to the unflavored product, to distinguish it from the many popular varieties of flavored and sweetened yogurt. Available made from whole, lowfat or nonfat milk.

Zest
Thin, brightly colored, outermost layer of a citrus fruit's peel, containing most of its aromatic essential oils—a lively source of flavor.

Zest may be removed with a small hand-held grater for very fine gratings; with a simple tool known as a zester (below), drawn across the fruit's skin to remove the zest in thin shreds;

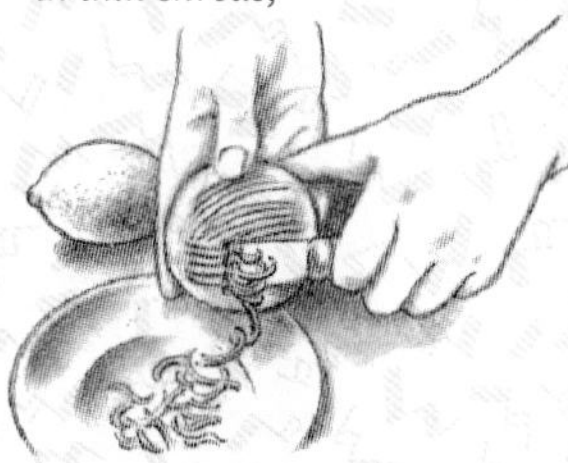

or in wide strips with a vegetable peeler (below) or a paring knife held almost parallel to the fruit's skin. Zest removed with the latter two tools may then be thinly sliced or chopped on a cutting board.

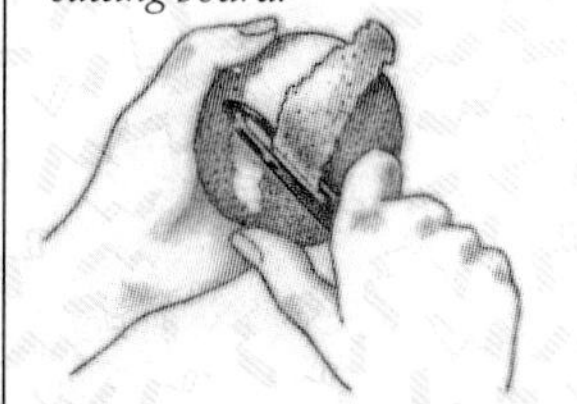

Index

Acknowledgments

The publishers would like to thank the following people and organizations for their generous assistance and support in producing this book:
William Garry, Kristine Kidd, Todd Taverner, Henry and Nancy Tenaglia, Annie and Mike Denn, Maria and Chris Watson, Sharon C. Lott, Stephen W. Griswold, Ken DellaPenta, Stephani Grant, Tina Schmitz, Marguerite Ozburn, the buyers and store managers for Pottery Barn and Williams-Sonoma stores.

The following kindly lent props for the photography: Biordi Art Imports, Candelier, Fillamento, Forrest Jones, Fredericksen Hardware, Mariner & Myers Flowers, Sue Fisher King, RH Shop, and Chuck Williams.

WILLIAMS-SONOMA
GRANDE CUISINE